To:_____

From:_____

THE WHOLE HEART OF

ZEN

THE COMPLETE TEACHINGS FROM THE ORAL TRADITION OF TA-MO

The Whole Heart of™ Zen
Copyright © 2006 by Fey Family Wu-Su, Inc.
New Forest® is a registered trademark of Fey Family Wu-Su, Inc.
Book design by Pat Covert
Calligraphy by Rev. John A. Bright-Fey

"The Whole Heart of" is a trademark of Crane Hill Publishers, Inc.

ISBN-13: 978-1-57587-233-9
ISBN-10: 1-57587-233-1

Published by Crane Hill Publishers
www.cranehill.com

Printed in China

Library of Congress Cataloging-in-Publication Data

Bright-Fey, J. (John)
  The whole heart of Zen / translation and commentary by John A. Bright-Fey.
      p. cm.
   ISBN-13: 978-1-57587-233-9
   1. Bodhidharma, 6th cent. 2. Spiritual life–Zen Buddhism. I. Title.
   BQ9299.B627B75 2006
   294.3'927–dc22

                                    2006005294

THE WHOLE HEART OF

ZEN

THE COMPLETE TEACHINGS FROM THE ORAL TRADITION OF TA-MO

REVEREND VENERABLE
JOHN BRIGHT-FEY

CRANE HILL
PUBLISHERS

BUDDHA

DEDICATION AND ACKNOWLEDGMENTS

This book brings to light the heretofore-secret oral literature of ancient China. It seems only fitting that those individuals who kept the tradition alive be acknowledged for their efforts. Therefore, I dedicate this book to the Dharma Mind Seal Lineage Holders of the Blue Dragon Order of Esoteric Zen Buddhism. These individuals devoted themselves to the preservation of the old in the ever-changing face of the new.

Kwan Ng Lo (1524 - ?): Founder/Warrior/Innocent
P'ang Ben Yu
P'ang Shih Yu
Ma Tin Hwa
Sung Nin Jan
Meng Cho Yao
Fei Tzu Lin
Sun Lok
Lo Ng Gao
Sun Ma Hao
Chi Wing Chow

John Bright-Fey: Current Lineage Holder

Thank you for reminding us that we stand on the shoulders of giants.

TABLE OF CONTENTS

THE WHOLE HEART OF ZEN

INTRODUCTION

As the rain and the snow come down from heaven, and do not return to it without watering the earth and making it bud and flourish, so that it yields seed for the sower and bread for the eater, so is my word that goes out of my mouth: It will not return to me empty, but will accomplish what I desire and achieve the purpose for which I sent it.

Isaiah 55:10-11 (NIV)

Thirty years ago, I was fortunate enough to participate in several Native American sweat-lodge rituals. "Sweats," as they are called, can last for hours or even days depending upon the tribal organizers. These are marvelous spiritual events. Through a combination of ritual purification, silent meditation, drumming, and chanted hymns, the soul is made more receptive to the Great Mystery. Visions are commonplace, as are intuitive insights into all facets of life. Awash in flashes of intuition and holy trance, the participants of a sweat make contact with their motive force of living and their highest happiness. A close friend introduced me to this spiritual practice. He was the grandson of a tribal Medicine Chief enamored of Asian philosophy. His grandfather and I became fast friends the very first time we met.

One particular evening, our usual silent communion with the Unseen gave rise to a series of spontaneous recitations of Indian tribal song and story. At one point, the Chief requested that I "sing my song of my elders." I proceeded to recite selections from the *Tao Te Ching*, Buddhist sutras, and even several of my favorite Sung dynasty poems. Some I declaimed in Chinese and others in English. I even managed to sing some of them in the fashion of my fellow participants. The polite smiles I received reminded me of the true purpose of our gathering, to reaffirm our sense of brotherhood with all creation.

At the conclusion of the sweat, I was asked to recite more oral wisdom from the ancient Chinese. There, surrounding a blazing fire in the Oklahoma outback, I recited Ta-Mo's "Sermon on the Correct Practice of Zen."

When I had finished, my friend declared that I should write the sermon down and have it published. His grandfather shot him an intense disapproving glare and said, "What's wrong with you? Do you not have the mind to memorize those words or the heart to recite them? How can you expect to ever stand upon the brink of eternity and share what you've learned in life?" Everyone in the circle sat silently for what seemed like forever. My friend, stung by his grandfather's rebuke, silently stared into the fire. Finally, the old Chief broke the silence saying, "The power is in the telling, the hearing, and the telling again." Indeed.

Speech—oral language—is one of man's greatest glories. Please understand that I am not referring to literacy. Linguistics, or "speaking" culture, is completely different from the subculture of the written word. After all, alphabets, characters, and written words are latecomers in the history of human language. I believe that there is a primordial connection to the spoken word that does not readily exist in the written. The words that we learn in school and that adorn the pages of books (like this one) are, fundamentally, dried out. There is no life in them; they are only made of paper. Yet, for some crazy reason, we tend to give these dead things more weight than the living word. Why is that? Just because a person can read and write doesn't mean that they are, somehow, superior to those who cannot. Yet, all too often, that's precisely how we behave.

Let me be as clear as I am able; reading and writing do, indeed, have many uses. I celebrate them. But it is undeniable that when education is introduced into an oral culture with its own unique oral literature and personality, it suffers. Unfortunately, the oral culture is often destroyed altogether. Dependence upon the written word easily takes the place of memory, discipline, recitation, personal transmission, and the societal structures that support them. Memory, as a vital part of oral tradition, becomes the poor cousin to intellect and mind. Why memorize when you can read? Why should you commit a stirring speech to memory when you can watch a video recording of the person making it? Why memorize a poem when you can push a button and play a recording of it? Why should you be expected to remember the dates of historical events, multiplication tables, the periodic table of elements, logarithms, or the names of the bones in the human body when a computer or calculator is easily available? Saint Augustine believed that memory was a divine gift that existed to remind man of his heavenly origin. With the advances of recording, printing, and computer technology comes the threat that the magic art of memory—the spark of the Almighty within each of us— will be extinguished. Sadly, with the loss of the divine spark of memory comes the inevitable extinction of the oral tradition. Zen Buddhism is one of those oral traditions that, I feel, is at risk.

The historic Buddha knew about man's predilection for confusing the written word with the spoken one. He knew, and even remarked, that even his spoken words would be misunderstood the very instant they left his lips. But, the Buddha also knew the power of the spoken word and endeavored to keep his message an orally transmitted one. To that end, he forbade the writing down of his Dharma, insisting, instead, in the rote memorization of its laws and precepts. Further, he emphasized the importance of direct human contact when transmitting Buddhist truth. In so doing, he established one of the longest unbroken person-to-person wisdom traditions in human history.

When the Buddha died, written words about Buddhism were few and no statues of him existed to be venerated. By the time of Ta-Mo, more than a thousand years later, the situation was quite different. Statues and icons of the Buddha were near ubiquitous, and the East Indian Buddhist Canon was nothing short of ponderous. Ta-Mo, the Twenty-Eighth Buddhist Patriarch, firmly believed that a complete awareness of the sacred could only be transmitted orally. Yet, even inspired speech had its limitations and pitfalls. Words, if properly used, can bring a person to Enlightenment. Words used improperly can drive it from you.

All of this is important because an oral tradition requires a living representative to insure the clean transmission of the spiritual signal. Yet, books on Zen abound in every imaginable form. True, the rich spiritual heritage of the Buddhists is recorded for posterity in these volumes, but the personal relationship and direct transmission of the Zen Way is missing. By itself, this situation is not terribly egregious. When the student is ready, the teacher will appear. The dilemma, as I see it, is that too many of today's commentators on the subject of Zen speak and write on the subject from a position that doesn't merely neglect the oral culture of Zen, but ignores it altogether. This leads to speculation (or worse, pontification) on aspects of Zen history, technique, and culture that is, frankly, beyond the data available to them. To an intellectual, separating the oral literature from the written as a means of focusing on the printed word can be expedient. But, it ultimately creates a false picture of Zen.

Any spiritual life or practice that is worthy of the name requires time and discipline that few are willing to give. The opportunities for competent Zen training are not as plentiful as one would like. Then there is the devotional factor. Reading a book on Zen is so much easier than actually sitting in formal meditation, for example. I have always found it delightfully amusing that experienced Zen teachers, historically, have warned students about the perils of reading. "Don't allow a book to come between you and your Original Self," the saying goes. In some cases, Zen Masters actually forbade the reading of written material on Zen. In effect, a student's progress was not judged by how many Buddhist sutras he had read, but on how many he avoided reading!

Many academics are understandably wary of the spoken record, seeing it as inherently unreliable. To be sure, even spoken language can naturally degenerate over time. Disease, disaster, foreign incursion, trade, and exploration can result in all manner of tribal forgetfulness and revisionism. Changes in spoken language can—and often do— subvert the written. But, I think it's important to remember that, particularly in the case of Zen, the two evolved together and any discussion of Zen must give the oral equal prominence with the written. Failure to do so skews the outcome of any examination, no matter how well intentioned. Simply put, to only examine the conventionally accepted written record is to miss, at the very least, half of the target. To the authentic Zen practitioner, an examination of this kind is nothing short of intellectual materialism that buries the message deeper instead of uncovering it. How is one to deal with this situation, if one is to deal with it at all? What's a Zen Master to do?

If this is beginning to sound polemical, I apologize. Plainly, I feel that once conventional education is introduced to a tribe firmly grounded in the oral tradition, the tribe gets, well, "dumber" regarding the substance of the oral tradition. I see it as a loss of unique wisdom at the expense of common literacy. That having been said, I am not overly concerned. Every community is resilient and organic, shifting and changing to meet the demands of the age. What's important, at least in the Zen oral tradition, is that it should change and shift! In point of fact, Ta-Mo specifically designed his spiritual method so as to allow for immediate adaptation whenever it was required. He also built in safeguards that protect the student in his mystic explorations and search for the Buddha Mind. The Zen of Ta-Mo, taken in total, is a marvelous, highly developed, and refined spiritual technology. But it cannot be taken in total without a working knowledge of Zen's methods, perspectives, and philosophy that are contained only in the oral record. In an ideal situation, you would be hearing these sermons delivered by a Zen priest within the ritual of direct transmission. You would not be reading them in this, or any, book. But, the pace and shape of our modern culture presents a situation that, I feel, is anything but ideal. Consequently, I believe that adaptation is required if Zen is to continue to thrive. Hence, the book you now hold in your hands.

The orally transmitted words of the East Indian that would become the First Patriarch of Chinese Zen are not random stories and anecdotes. They are specific instructions in the cultivation of Zen and the Zen lifestyle.

The sermons in this volume represent a small portion of a much larger body of Zen oral literature. This body of Zen oral folklore has infused the minds, bodies, and fiery spirits of countless numbers of listeners for almost fifteen hundred years. The telling, the listening, and the retelling that have taken place over generations have evolved into a sophisticated method of speaking directly to our essential nature, that very same essential nature that the Buddha wanted each of his followers to discover for themselves. To perceive your essential nature and see your original face is to stand on the threshold of awakening. This is the Zen Buddhist ideal and the one to which this book is dedicated.

On that dark Oklahoma night, I was aghast at the thought of committing to page and ink what I had already committed to blood and memory. To write it down seemed, to me, a sacrilege. Now, older and hopefully wiser, I present to you the orally transmitted sermons of Ta-Mo, the founder of Zen Buddhism. For many generations, these poems have been kept a closely guarded secret. Each of them was transmitted to me within the strict ritual of the Buddhist contemplative and lineage holder. No written text was used. Likewise, all of the information contained in each commentary is from the oral record. I relied on nothing, save the spoken word of my teacher just as he had relied on the spoken words of his. I learned these sermons during long hours of call and response. Much like the Taoist tradition, which makes the act of memorization a mystic event, the use of mindful labor, symbolic gesture, and transformative martial movement were vital parts of the entire esoteric process. It is my hope that these printed sermons and the commentary that accompanies them will cut through both the academic and pop-culture haze that has currently gathered around the subject of authentic Zen practice.

ON THIS TRANSLATION

There is no simple and direct way to substitute one English word for a single Chinese word. Instead, most of the words used in these sermons can represent many English words and concepts. It is only through the actual practice of Zen that one can determine what is authentic and what is ersatz. The language that Ta-Mo employs is particularly nuanced and complex. Due to the very nature of Zen, it abounds in both natural and deliberate paradox. Much of the language has a depth of meaning with many subsidiary meanings "beneath" its predominant one. This is also true of the English language, but few of us are normally aware of it.

I've also chosen to use the Japanese term "Zen" instead of the more accurate Chinese term "Ch'an" throughout this book. I do this because the word "Zen" enters the English reader's consciousness more easily than its Chinese counterpart. Likewise, I have tried to use Indian and Chinese words sparingly. It is my hope that you will get the wisdom contained in these sermons "under your fingertips" as soon as possible. To that end, I want nothing—particularly the unfamiliarity of a foreign word—to stand in your way. I hope that you will understand my reasoning.

For this translation, I've chosen to use capital letters and punctuation even though none are readily apparent during oral recitation. The choices of poetic structure are my own. They reflect the cadence, feel, and rhythm I employ when I recite these sermons aloud. To my knowledge, this is the first time that this particular transmission has had this kind of structure imposed on it. It is my hope that the choices I've made will be successful in translating ancient Chinese oral poetic form into a contemporarily relevant structure for English readers. This is a tall order, to be sure. Taking the time to read these cantos aloud will, I trust, help you get even closer to the Zen messages contained in the words themselves.

This presentation of the sermons of Ta-Mo will be accompanied by a detailed exposition into its dynamics. The commentary that follows each of the cantos will explain the inner workings of each. Traditionally, Zen Masters have relied on the spoken force of a complete canto rather than focusing on separate stanzas. I have attempted to shape my comments accordingly. The comments themselves will be classified in four ways:

The Zen Mind: This reflects the proper mindset and worldview of the traditional Zen Cultivator. Simply put, these comments outline precisely how a Zen Buddhist thinks.

The Zen Body: These comments will address the day-to-day concerns of living a Zen Buddhist life.

The Zen Hand: Comments under this heading concern the actual training and devotional techniques employed by a Cultivator of the Zen Way. These techniques establish the spiritual discipline of the Zen Buddhist.

The Zen Heart: Comments under this heading reflect Zen core beliefs. More simply put, these are the things that a Zen Buddhist holds dear.

It will be obvious as you read that many of my comments overlap from one heading to another. This is intentional. Overlapping concerns and principles abound in many of the worlds' great philosophical traditions, and Zen is no different.

The sermons that I've chosen for this volume are the ones that I have personally found most important in my own life. Aficionados will, at times, feel familiar ground beneath their feet. More often, I suspect, this presentation will break new ground as it leads you into uncharted territory.

Most other currently available translations of Ta-Mo's sermons are wonderful in their own way. However, they come from the written record and not the Zen oral tradition. As such, they only succeed in delivering the cargo, so to speak. All too often, when the cargo arrives, it is damaged. Centuries of sectarian infighting, endless commentaries, copying and recopying of handwritten manuscripts have all contributed to this damage. None of these translations, in my view, adequately reflects the force and power of Zen oral culture. As such, they fall short of presenting a complete picture of the Zen of Ta-Mo. This volume seeks to remedy the situation. In my view, the time is right for these sermons to enjoy a wider audience. It is my belief that the world can benefit greatly from the wisdom contained within them.

The sermons you are about to read come from the oral literature of The Blue Dragon Order of Esoteric Zen Buddhism, known in Chinese as *Lamm Loong Pac*. It is representative of a vast memorized archive of spiritual knowledge and wisdom. It is my sincerest hope that you find it useful as you walk your chosen path in life.

John Bright-Fey, Zen Master
Reverend Venerable, Tao-jen, Tao-shih

MIND

BODY

HAND

HEART

SERMON ONE

SERMON ON
CORRECT PRACTICE

CANTO I

Hear me!
These are words that bind time, itself.
These are words that flow from the Buddha Mind.
I have heard them and, now, so shall you.
Hear me!

I will speak to you
On the correct practice of Zen.

COMMENTARY

Zen Mind: The goal of Zen study is not the mere understanding of its teachings but, rather, a direct and instant experience of cosmic reality known as sudden awakening, or *tun-wu*. The concept of sudden awakening is one of the main differences between the Buddhism of India and China. The attainment of enlightenment can be achieved either quickly or gradually in the Zen tradition, depending upon the student's individual gifts and deficits. That having been said, Ta-Mo preached and taught with a primary emphasis on seeing your "original face" and gaining enlightenment instantly. As a consequence, sudden awakening became a vital part of the Zen mindset. Many methods evolved to engineer this awakening. Among them were loud shouts and gestures that were designed to grab the attention and shock the student into spiritual wakefulness. During the oral transmission of this sermon, the first and fifth lines are delivered in a loud and demanding manner providing those in attendance an opportunity to grasp the cosmic reality and, spiritually, wake up.

Zen Body: Buddhist monks and students attending a recitation of Ta-Mo's sermons were required to listen contemplatively, or "attend to the words and allow your mind to rest upon them." In brief, contemplative listening involves being mindfully aware of the recitation while attempting to hear it with the entire being. Contemplative practice of this kind is a mainstay of everyday activity for the Zen Buddhist monk who attempts to live life in a state of elevated awareness and complete mindfulness.

Zen Hand: Rather than being abstract discussions of Buddhist dogma, the sermons of Ta-Mo are recognized as succinct and clear instructions on the practice of meditation. In fact, in and of itself, each sermon is considered to be a profound meditation.

Zen Heart: It is a Zen core belief that the Buddha is an eternal being that binds time and is the embodiment of universal wisdom and cosmic truth. The Buddha neither lives nor dies but exists across eternity. As needed, the Buddha manifests in the ordinary realm as an historical person in order to lead people away from suffering and to salvation. The incarnated Buddha transmits the Dharma, or teachings, which flow from a universal source and ground of being known as the Buddha Mind.

CANTO II

A great many roads lead to the Tao—
The Zen Way of Life.
But though they exist in multitude, great variety, and
    great numbers,
These roads have only two faces.
The first is the face of transcendental reason and
    understanding:
That is,
To enter the Way by higher intuition and mystic sense.
The second is the face of transcendental practice:
That is,
To gain entrance into the Way through inspired
    practical living.

Repeat after me:
Reason,
Practice.

COMMENTARY

Zen Mind: The philosophy of Taoism greatly affected the Buddhism that came from India. In fact, it was the confluence of indigenous Chinese philosophy and mainstream Indian Buddhism that figured prominently in the unique birth of the Zen approach. During the time of Ta-Mo, the word Tao and Zen (*Ch'an*) were used interchangeably. Oral tradition holds that Ta-Mo frequently employed Chinese philosophical terminology so as to allow Buddhist concepts to more readily enter the Chinese consciousness. For their part, the Chinese regarded the Buddhist religion as an Indian form of Taoism and, initially at least, saw little difference between the two.

Zen Body: The Zen Way of Life was an extension of the Mahayana school of Buddhism from which it came. Mahayana Buddhism, also known as the Great Vehicle, derived from Theravada Buddhism, known as the Law of the Elders. Theravada, also known as Primitive or Canonical Buddhism, is essentially an individual discipline of personal salvation. This salvation was possible only if the adherent firmly and completely rejected the everyday world and joined the monastic order. The monastic goal was to become a perfect saint, or *arhat*. Traditionally, the Theravada *arhat* was an aloof, cold, and detached individual who removed himself from society. Though part of a monastic order, the practice of his religion was a solitary one. Any accumulated spiritual merit remained his and his alone.

In rebellion to the narrow and exclusionary practices of Theravada, a new Buddhist school emerged that offered spiritual salvation to everyone, rather than a few select individuals. This was the Mahayana. It emphasized charity and compassion for all sentient beings, and love of your fellow man. Self-sacrifice was elevated to a devotional practice. Further, it taught that individual spiritual endeavors benefited everyone. These beliefs were in direct contrast to Canonical Buddhism, which the Mahayanists called Hinayana, or the Small Vehicle.

In the main, Buddhists who embrace the Zen Way of Life govern their day-to-day activities according to the precepts of the large vehicle.

Zen Hand: Entering the Way requires dedication and hard work. Entering through the face of reason generally results in sudden awakening, while entering through inspired living is associated with gradual awakening. This is not to say, however, that gradual awakening is easier and/or more accessible than sudden awakening. Inspired living can establish a firm spiritual foundation

for an adherent who has none. But at some point, a true
Zen Buddhist must learn to engage higher intuition and
mystic sense. This can only be achieved by meditation.

Zen Heart: The Zen Way is an uncomplicated one.
Yet, there appear to be a great many kinds of practice.
The reason for the great variety of Zen practice is
because it has changed and adapted over the years to
fit the various populations that embrace it. But no matter
what form it takes, as long as it reflects either
transcendental reason or practice, Zen philosophy holds
that enlightenment can be achieved in one's lifetime.

CANTO III

TRANSCENDENTAL REASONING

To enter the Tao,
The Zen Way of Life,
With the face of transcendental reason and understanding
Is to clearly realize the Zen Essence through direct
    transmission and,
By this instruction,
Intrinsically believe
That all living things share the same essential nature;
That is, the same *qi*;
The same life force.

All that lives is a balance of the Way.
Expressive, receptive;
Vital, unimportant;
Destructive, creative—this is the *yin* and *yang*.
Make no mistake.
All things
Are
All these things.

COMMENTARY

Zen Mind: The idea of clarity, or *ching*, is a fundamental component of Zen. As meditation deepens, the consciousness of the practitioner is purified and self-realization becomes possible. The Zen Master possesses more clarity than the novice and is able to clearly see, precisely, what needs to occur for the student to become realized. Knowing what to say or do to bring increasing levels of clarity to the student is part of the direct transmission process. The first step usually revolves around the concept that each individual part of creation is intimately connected to every other part of creation. This forms the beginning of Zen One-Pointedness.

Zen Body: Direct transmission is the Zen method of passing on the Buddhist teachings and precepts known as the Dharma. The Zen Buddhist tradition is a living tradition that has been passed down from one human being to another since the time of Shakyamuni, who became the historical Buddha. The direct transmission process entails person-to-person initiation. Said another way, Buddhism is a living tradition that has been passed down from one human being to another in an unbroken chain since 600 B.C.E.

Zen Hand: Meditation is the essential path to oneness with the Absolute, or *nirvana*. Oneness with the Absolute begins with the recognition of the unified nature of the world. Meditating on the shared essential nature of all things results in a state of mental balance and equilibrium that informs every part of the meditator's life.

Zen Heart: The idea that all sentient beings—in fact, all that exists—share the same essence is a fundamental part of the Zen worldview.

CANTO IV

This sameness is not readily apparent
Because it is obscured and shrouded by sensation, as
    well as
The delusions that result from these sensations.
Those beings who turn away from this delusion
And turn back to the face of reality;
Those beings who turn away from the bound world
And turn back to the boundless;
Those who meditate on walls that contain both the *yin*
    and the *yang*;
Those who meditate on the absence of the self and other;
Those who meditate on the oneness of the mortal and
    sage
Will find that there is neither self nor some other
    person or thing.
They will not be drugged and enslaved by words,
Spoken or written,
And will engage the mystic sense,
And will be in direct intuitive contact with reason itself.

Intelligence viewing intelligence;
Completely free of conceptual discrimination.
They will be unmoving, effortlessly entering

By non-action
Into the Way with the face of transcendental reason and
    understanding.
That is how we say it.

COMMENTARY

Zen Mind: Zen practice is a sophisticated art of self-observation in which we turn our attention inward to seek our true nature. Normally, however, our attention is directed outward to the mundane aspects of life. The mundane convinces us that we are separate from what we observe. Our neurology is complicit in this act as it divides experience into discreet and manageable components. Small divisions of mental separation and classification soon build to larger ones, until the entire bodymind is engaged in a furious process of critical comparison. Things are judged, one to another, and their qualities are assessed and evaluated. Our sense organs, which allow us to interface with the outside world, bombard us with ever increasing amounts of data. Our mind, guided by our individual gifts and deficits, endeavors to keep this cascade of information organized by imposing convenient and habitual ways of thinking upon us. In Buddhism, this is known as the Discriminating Mind. Zen aims to train the mind to turn away from the mundane aspects of life and embrace the supramundane.

Zen Body: Managing the mundane aspects of life can become so overwhelming as to shut us off from one another. The Zen method of realization through self-analysis and self-reflection remedies this situation. Authentic Zen practice will always generate a spontaneous outflowing of love, compassion, and sympathy for all that lives. This outflowing fundamentally changes our behavior and perception as we realize that all of our lives are inseparably linked. As our awareness of this intimate connection deepens, we come to know that everything we think or do affects others and, eventually, reverberates back upon us. This awareness informs every part of the Zen life.

Zen Hand: Disengaging the Discriminating Mind is the first order of business to the Zen meditator. Ta-Mo taught two primary methods of meditation: *zou-ch'an* (also, *tso-ch'an* and *zazen* in Japanese), which means seated meditation, and a moving meditation called *shih-pa lohan shou-ch'an*, which means the Eighteen Hands of the Saint meditation. He also allowed elements of two Taoist meditation techniques to become part of the Zen school. These are called *zou-wang* (also, *tso-wang*) and *jing-zou*. Both methods employ long periods of quiet sitting and self-reflection.

Both the seated and the moving meditations that Ta-Mo taught are divided into stages. The first stage aims at calming the bodymind and developing contemplative skill in mental concentration called the One-Pointed Mind, or *I-hsing san-mei*. This method, called Tathagata Zen, was the beginning method most commonly taught by the Buddha himself. It is a technique of generating a complete mindful awareness of the breath. It is also the method that the Buddha employed to achieve his own awakening. Once the bodymind is calmed and concentrated, the meditator is allowed to move on to the next stages of Zen meditation, where the mind is turned from the mundane to the supramundane.

Seated Meditation Techniques

Preliminaries

The Seat of Meditation: The meditative seat is the physical setting and attire for formal Zen practice. Choose a quiet and comfortable environment for your meditation where the air is fresh and the temperature moderate. Likewise, your clothing should be clean and comfortable and not restrict your breathing in any way. Ablutions and devotionals may be performed if you desire. A ritualized entrance to the Zen environment can be helpful but, strictly speaking, is unnecessary. Seated Zen requires meditation cushions or a chair. It can also cause slight but noticeable changes in body temperature.

In this event, a light blanket draped over the shoulders can be a useful part of your attire.

The Posture of Meditation: Strictly speaking, almost any physical posture may be used for Zen. The seated postures are, however, the most efficacious for the fledgling meditator. Ta-Mo taught Zen in either the Full Lotus or the Half Lotus posture. In the Full Lotus, the legs are crossed with the foot of the right leg resting on the left thigh and the left foot resting on the right thigh. The Half Lotus is formed by placing one foot on the opposite thigh and resting the other foot on the ground. If either of these is too difficult, you may rest both bent legs on the ground with one directly in front of the other.

Use cushions to insure that your hips are higher than your knees. It is important that you have a stable physical base. If sitting cross-legged is physically inappropriate for you, you may sit in a chair with your feet flat on the floor and knees slightly lower than your hips.

Keep your trunk upright and tuck your chin slightly inward. Relax your shoulders and generate a sense that you are being pulled upright by the crown of your head. It is important that you not lean forward or back nor to one side or the other.

Oral tradition holds that Ta-Mo preferred the Open Circle hand posture, or *mudra*. Once you are comfortably upright, place the back of the left hand atop the right palm and fingers. Touch the tips of the thumbs together forming an empty circle. Allow the joined hands to rest near the lower abdomen.

With the body stable and organized, the mind can be stabilized and organized, as well.

First Stage

The Tathagata Meditation Technique: Smile faintly. Traditionally, the eyes may be either closed or half-opened.

Bring your attention to the Lower Heaven, or *tan tien*. The *tan tien* is sometimes called The Golden Elixir Field of Cinnabar and is located three and one-half inches below your navel and inward toward the center of your lower abdomen.

Observe the rising and falling of the lower abdomen for five to ten minutes while maintaining light attention on the *tan tien*. This will calm your mind, boost your vitality, and focus your concentration.

Begin observing the length, depth, or quality of each inhalation and exhalation by judging it against pairs of opposites. Label each as either rough or smooth or, if you prefer, long or short. You might judge the breath as deep or shallow or even thick or thin. It is your choice. Merely choose a pair and maintain it for the duration of the meditative session. Employing a mental dialogue can be used as an aid to observation. For example, you may hear your inner voice saying, "I breathe in;... long. I breathe out;... long. I breathe in;... short" and so on.

Distractions will occur. When you find yourself thinking about anything other than judging your breath, smile faintly and say "thinking" with your inner voice. Immediately return to the process of observing and judging your breath. It is important not to feel badly about having been distracted. In point of fact, if you were not self-distracted, a meditation master would have to provide distractions for you. To be distracted when meditating, becoming aware of it, and gently returning to the object of your meditation is referred to in Tathagata Zen practice as Purifying Your Consciousness. It is an important part of achieving One-Pointedness.

Maintain mindful awareness of your breath for as long as you like. Allow both the breath and the process of observation to unfold naturally. Simply breathe quietly and calmly. Nothing else exists save you and your breath.

Over time, the meditator learns to effectively sweep distracting thoughts aside and merge completely with the object of meditation, in this case, the breath. This merging, palpably experienced as the entire bodymind flowing into the object of meditation, is classically called *samadhi* and *i-hsing san-mei*, or One-Pointedness. Ta-Mo referred to *samadhi* as the mystic sense. This is a fundamental skill necessary for progress as a Zen contemplative.

After the meditator begins acquiring the skill of maintaining *samadhi* during everyday activities, as well as during the Eighteen Hands, they may undertake the practice of Patriarch Zen.

Second Stage

The Patriarch Zen Technique (Part One): Assume a meditative posture and practice being mindfully aware of your breath until you begin to engage One-Pointed concentration.

As thoughts arise, rest your mystic sense upon them and investigate their origins. For example, when a distracting thought manifests in your consciousness, view it with One-Pointedness and ask yourself, "Where did this thought come from? What does it really mean? Why did it appear to me at this time?" etc. Make no judgments about the distracting thought. Rather, observe it to see where it came from. It is your job to deeply penetrate the distracting thought and any successive thoughts that gave rise to it as you, unerringly, trace it to its source. In Zen, this is called sweeping away thoughts.

Investigating the origins of errant thoughts yields increasing levels of intuitive insight concerning all manner of subjects, including the thoughts themselves. Continue this investigation for as long as you like.

The first part of Patriarch Zen is designed to yield a cascade of intuitive insight into the nature of the self, in particular, and existence, in general. At first, the cascade is unorganized and confused. But, if the meditator investigates them in a calm, concentrated, and deliberate manner, they become profoundly organized. As these cascades of intuitive insight become more organized, the Zen contemplative feels as if he has discarded his body and mind altogether. When this occurs, it is time to move on to the second part of Patriarch Zen.

The Patriarch Zen Technique (Part Two): When body and mind seem to vanish amid a steady stream of insights, distracting thoughts appear less often and the successive levels of each become fewer in number. At this point, the meditation takes on a spontaneous quality as deeper investigation draws you closer to a point where no thoughts arise at all. The meditation becomes free and unrestricted, as you are absorbed into the Boundless. Through no deliberate action of your own, you gain entrance into the Cosmic Reality. Zen refers to this realization as turning around to see your original face. It is a profound experience that, when nurtured, results in the continual process of self-realization actually becoming your Zen practice. This is entering the Way through transcendental reason and understanding.

Zen Heart: In the original Zen expounded at the Shaolin Temple, Ta-Mo referred to the mundane and supramundane as the Bound and the Boundless. The Bound, or *shih*, was the phenomenal world of consensual reality, as well as the activity of the discriminating mind that was responsible for creating it. Mental discipline engendered by the practice of Zen allows us to function more efficiently in the Bound world. It stimulates our intuition and breaches our habitual way of looking at things. All of this can be very beneficial to our day-to-day, but the spiritual goal is to move from the Bound to the Boundless, or *li*, where the normal habitual actions and reactions of our bodymind cease. At that point, we enter a state where the action of the discriminating mind yields to a state of non-action. This is the threshold of the Boundless. We have but to enter.

CANTO V

TRANSCENDENTAL PRACTICE:
THE FOUR PRACTICES

To enter the Way with the face of transcendental
    practice means
To enter the Tao through inspired practical living and
    conduct.

There are four practices in which all other acts are
    included.
These are:
Number one, learning how to requite injury, anger, and
    hatred;
Number two, learning how to follow and adapt to
    conditions;
Number three, learning how not to seek or crave anything;
Number four, learning how to practice the Dharma.

When each one of these practices is properly inspired
Becoming authentic and second nature
To you,
Then the face of transcendental reason and understanding
Will present itself.

COMMENTARY

Zen Mind: Progress in Zen takes time and energy. Formal Zen meditation leads to transcendental reason and understanding, which eventually culminates in awakening. While formal practice ripens, the insights gained through meditation spill over into everyday life. If the Zen contemplative lives his life inspired by the Zen Way, then the act of living in the consensual world becomes a kind of informal practice that accelerates his spiritual development. All of the Four Practices eventually lead to the development of the mystic sense, thereby ushering in the face of transcendental reason and understanding.

Zen Body: The principles of inspired practical living and conduct reflect the accumulated wisdom of the Zen tradition. Authentic Zen practice naturally generates respect and love for our fellow man. The methods of conduct allow us to focus and apply this beneficence as a way of honoring it.

Zen Hand: It is useful to think of following the principles of inspired living and conduct as a kind of formula for enlightenment. However, if your behavior becomes mechanical, then your efforts will be wasted. In truth, the principles of transcendental practice should manifest naturally within you. Your experience must be authentic. It's as if you naturally follow the precepts of inspired living without anyone having to tell you what they are. In essence, you create them spontaneously.

Zen Heart: The desire to respect, protect, and love our fellow man is a central belief in Zen Buddhism. If the feelings are authentic, they flow from the heart of the contemplative directly to the hearts of those around him. This was a primary focus at the Shaolin Temple where Zen was founded. Each monk was required to recreate himself on a daily basis by personally finding new ways to understand the art of transcendental practice.

CANTO VI

REQUITING INJURY, ANGER, AND HATRED

What is meant by the conduct of requiting injury,
    anger, and hatred?
You must learn to balance the blind momentum and
    energy of each.
When people who search for the Tao encounter difficulty
And have to struggle through adverse conditions,
They should think to themselves,
"In countless ages gone by, I have been many
    people in many guises.
I have wandered through a multiplicity of existences,
All the while concerning myself with the trivial
And unimportant details of life
At the expense of the essentials of life.
I have often been angry without a reason,
Creating infinite occasions of injury, anger, and hatred."
These are all imbalances of the Tao.

COMMENTARY

Zen Mind: Bodymind balance is essential to the Zen mindset. Nothing can disturb this balance more than anger, hatred, and the injurious activity that flows from them. Understanding the roots of hatred and anger is a way to reestablish mental and physical equilibrium.

Zen Body: The most profound idea that extends from this canto and the two that follow is the notion that you can confront your own propensity to be fearful and angry without allowing yourself to be frozen by overwhelming feelings of guilt. This perspective begins to blunt the force of adverse conditions.

Zen Hand: Ta-Mo's injunctions throughout this sermon apply not only to managing your life according to the principles of Zen. They also apply to managing formal meditation practice. How you conduct yourself in the consensual and Bound world is precisely how you should conduct yourself in the Boundless.

Zen Heart: While most Buddhists of Ta-Mo's time believed that it takes many lifetimes to stop the momentum of disharmony, known as Karma, Zen adherents held that the karmic wheel could be stilled in one human chronological lifetime. That one lifetime, however, could also be one phase of life. If approached properly, a single phase of life can be lived as a chronological one with Zen awakening punctuating its end. Then, the adherent can move into the next phase of his life under the profound influence of the Way.

CANTO VII

Even though I am no longer committing these
   violations of the Way,
The momentum and energy of the violations is still
   affecting me.
Why is this?
Disharmony of the past creates disharmony of the present.
Neither gods nor men can truly foretell
What will happen to their own selves, much less to me.
Who can say when or in what form this disharmony will
   manifest itself?

Whatever form it takes,
I will accept it as an opportunity with an open heart,
   willingly and patiently.
I will not indulge in sadness.
I will not scream "Injustice!"

COMMENTARY

Zen Mind: The Zen mind is stabilized by willfully embracing a state of pleasant insecurity. Ruminating over the reasons for misfortune is an emotional wringing of hands. Without indulging in the pain created by violations of the Way, accept bad happenings as an opportunity to see your essential nature. This is Zen.

Zen Body: Most of us live life as if we are supposed to be omniscient. But if we live life as an adventure—not knowing what is coming next—we can begin to requite anger, hatred, and injury.

Zen Hand: As you pacify your mind, it can rebelliously produce very negative thoughts. When a distracting thought arises during meditation, accept it with an open heart no matter what form it takes.

Zen Heart: Suffering, or *dukha*, occurs when we grasp at and hold onto pain and negative feelings. It's as if we are a conduit for feelings and sensations that have become clogged with tiny rocks and other obstructions. As the pain moves through us, it is blocked, compressed, and trapped within. This is the Zen meaning of indulgence.

CANTO VIII

The sutra is a written thread tied to the essence of
    wisdom.
It passes through and manifests itself in humankind.
It binds our essential nature together.
One important thread of wisdom states,
"Don't be upset when you meet with adversity or other
    ills.
Why?
Because things are overseen,
Surveyed by a higher intelligence alive with causation:
Disharmony makes sense."
Here the thread ends.
With such an understanding, you will be in accord
    with transcendental reason
And will understand how to balance blind
    momentum and energy.
Then you will requite injury, anger, and hatred.
Through this understanding of disharmony,
You will, eventually, enter the Way with the face of
    transcendental reason.

COMMENTARY

Zen Mind: Ta-Mo referred to Zen as "a unique and secret transmission that exists outside of the scriptures and does not rely on words or letters." He did, however, quote selectively from older Buddhist texts known as *sutra* or *sutta*. *Sutras* are the physical manifestations of continuous streams of the Buddha Mind that have existed across time.

Zen Body: Requiting injury, anger, and hatred with acts of love and compassion is the Zen Way to balance out disharmony. Simply put, when you feel bad, do something nice for someone else.

Zen Hand: As a practical manner, you are an extension of the higher intelligence. The model for inspired living and conduct is the manner in which you conduct self-investigation during meditation.

Zen Heart: Disharmony, pain, anger, and all manner of negativity is an outgrowth of the deluded and unbalanced mind. The only way out of this delusion is to understand that whatever we think or do, for good or ill, affects the entire universe.

CANTO IX

ADAPTING TO CONDITIONS

What is meant by "following and adapting to
    conditions"?
As mortals, we are ruled by conditions and not by
    our natural self.
The wisdom-thread states that
"There is no self in beings past, present, or future.
They have been created out of the interplay of the
    energies of Karma.
The pleasure I feel is the result of previous actions.
The pain I feel is the result of previous actions.
Both are the fruit of a seed I planted long ago.
When the karmic energies have been exhausted,
The conditions change and the fruit no longer exists."

Why should I be happy and sad over this?
Success and failure depend on a variety of conditions,
But, the mind,
The mind knows neither increase nor decrease: It is
    constant.
Those who are unmoved by the winds of pain,
Those who are not shaken by the winds of pleasure

Are in silent harmony with the Tao
And enter the Way with the face of transcendental
  reason.

COMMENTARY

Zen Mind: In the ancient Indian Buddhist texts, Karma is a blind machine and almost totally malevolent. Ta-Mo taught that Karma is the energy of any human action that, like ripples created by tossing a stone into a pond, extends outward across time and space from the action itself. This was a fundamental reordering of Buddhist thought associated with the Mahayana. The Buddhists of China before Ta-Mo, though sincere, wrestled with the idea of Karma but failed to grasp its subtleties. Ta-Mo arrived and remedied this situation by passing on the Mind Seal of Buddhism that forms the core of Zen.

Zen Body: All beings are, fundamentally, benevolent and naturally awakened. Unfortunately, the deluded mind blocks our essential nature and separates us from harmony. Even our concept of self is created by the confused, grasping, and deluded mind. Adapting to conditions, when practically applied, is accomplished by self-observation. During normal activities, observe your reactions to things as mindfully as possible. See the mind as a mirror that reflects any reaction, either good or bad, and treat each with equal importance. This is the practice of equanimity. Each reaction you have should be regarded as not any more or less important as any other reaction. In this way, your daily actions will mimic the actions of the Original Mind.

Zen Hand: Treating activities, thoughts, and reactions with equanimity involves what I call the Three D's, namely, Delicate, Distance, and Deference. In practice, regard every reaction as a fragile thing that could break, change, or shift at any moment. Attempt to emotionally and mentally pull back from it to see it in its totality. Make no guesses or judgments about the reaction and allow it to unfold on its own without your interference. This principle applies to both formal Zen practice and the informal practice of living a Zen life.

Zen Heart: Adapting to conditions can be thought of as adhering to and following the terms of a contract. The contract in question is the search for the Buddha Mind that we all possess, as well as the delusions that inevitably result as a consequence of our mortality. Simply put, we are all naturally spiritual beings having mortal experiences in order to fully grasp and complete our divine Buddha Nature.

CANTO X

SEEK AND CRAVE NOTHING

What is meant by "not seeking or craving anything"?
People of this world are in chaos and confusion.
They are attached to one thing or another,
This or that idea,
Always seeking or craving something.
This is the sleep of ignorance.
Only mystic wisdom can truly awaken you
To choose the face of reason over everyday customs and
    habits.

Serenely and resolutely focus your mind on the
    uncreated
And abide in the Tao.
Let your bodymind move about according to the
    causal energies of nature,
Mimicking the changes and flux of the seasons.

All phenomena are linked to the Void,
And, by this nature, are empty.
Therefore, there is nothing in them that can be sought or
    desired.
Yin and *yang* exist together.

Brightness and darkness are, indeed, each other.
Both have their place.

COMMENTARY

Zen Mind: The consensual world of experienced phenomena is called *samsara*. It is our normal mode of existence characterized by our painful attachment to desires and illusions. *Nirvana*, on the other hand, is the act of moving into a new mode of existence blissfully free from attachment, seeking, and craving. In Zen thought, *samsara* and *nirvana* form an essential unity of emptiness. *Samsara* is *nirvana* and *nirvana* is *samsara*. If you are unenlightened, then the world is *samsara*. If, however, you are enlightened, then the world is *nirvana*. It all depends upon your state of mind.

Zen Body: Attachment can be thought of as a complicated series of obsessions and conclusions that lead you away from the essence of authentic life. Rationalizations are attachments, as are prejudices and habits. If the manner and quality of your interaction with people, events, and things comes from this place, your experience is said to be inauthentic. Your attachments, not your true self, are governing your experience of life.

The goal of Zen living is to relate to the world's true nature and not its phenomenal aspects.

Zen Hand: Applying one-pointed concentration and intuitive insight is the Zen method of dissolving attachments. Allowing the mind to rest on a specific prejudice, fear, habit, or rationalization is the first step. Thereafter, the Zen Cultivator intuitively probes the attachment as a bodymind construct. Sensations, memories, and other mind-stuff that is connected to the construct become ancillary objects of Zen meditation. Eventually, the Cultivator gains intimate wisdom and deep insight into the root cause of the attachment. All of this intimate wisdom is revealed intuitively.

Zen Heart: *Nirvana* and *samsara* are two sides of the same coin. At the core of each is the same essence that is nothingness. Because Zen philosophy holds all experienced phenomena as fundamentally empty, including *nirvana* and *samsara*, any intellectual examination is pointless.

CANTO XI

We all live in this limited existence.
This is referred to as the Three Worlds.
And we have lived in this blazing house for far too long.

We all live in these bodyminds, which, as a matter
    of existence,
Must suffer.
Who can deny that we suffer due to the very
    existence of natural forces?
All that has a bodymind will experience friction and
    suffering and,
As a consequence, cannot be at total peace.
It is a fact.
No one with a bodymind, who is outside the Way,
    can know peace.

The wise person is completely aware
Of the good sense of this message and, therefore,
Will detach themselves from all things that are
    subject to change;
That is, all that exists.
Both as a consequence and as a method,
Their thoughts are quieted and they seek nothing.

An ancient wisdom-thread states, "When craving exists,
    pain follows.
When you seek after nothing, you are blessed."
By seeking nothing, you enter the Way with the
    face of transcendental reason.

COMMENTARY

Zen Mind: The Zen Buddhist concept of *dukha* is usually translated into English as suffering. This is a limited definition that, invariably, evokes Judeo-Christian parallels that do not reflect the Zen Way, i.e. suffering as a consequence of sin, etc. The best way to understand *dukha*, from Ta-Mo's perspective, is to think of it as the friction created by the energy of phenomenal experience as it moves through us. If the experience moves easily through us, we will not experience suffering. If, however, we restrict the force and energy of the experience by focusing on it, then suffering will result. For example, the Zen Master can experience anger without suffering because he allows the force and energy of the emotion to easily pass through his bodymind. Someone who is not as skilled invariably holds onto the feelings and sensations of anger until they build up and sink into his tissues and bones, as it were.

Zen Body: Accepting the inevitability of suffering as part of human experience, as well as experience in general, informs the Zen Way of Life. As a rule, Zen adherents are not as controlled by their suffering. For example, they may still experience pain and sickness. But, rather than focusing upon the inevitability of aging or mortality, they merely regard their pain or illness as one of the many mysteries of the human organism. This does not mean that they must ignore the pain or illness and passively live with it. Healing may still be sought. It is their unique relationship to the reality of the problem that is managed according to Zen philosophy.

Zen Hand: Detaching from all things that change is often mistaken as an injunction to remove oneself from family and society. Worse still, some impair their senses in such a way as to not experience anything at all. Authentic Zen detachment implies suspending your normal reactions to things that change and observing them as they naturally unfold before you.

Zen Heart: The Three Worlds is a metaphysical concept Ta-Mo borrowed from the Taoists that reflects the Taoist notion that the world of man joins the heavenly and earthly worlds. These are the worlds of consensual reality and phenomenal experience. From Ta-Mo's perspective, this was a model of the universe that was necessarily limited and did not adequately reflect the Universal Essence at the heart of the Absolute or Boundless.

CANTO XII

PRACTICING THE DHARMA

What is meant by learning how to practice the Dharma?
To practice the Dharma is to embrace the Way.
The Way determines our true essence.
Thus, it is the teaching that represents the universal truth.
This truth existed before the Buddha,
Who, like us, was merely a manifestation of the Way.

All nature in its essence is pure.
That which seems full is empty.
Defilements and attachments do not exist.
There is no self.
There is no form or shape.
There is no other.
There is no subject and no object.

COMMENTARY

Zen Mind: Followers of Zen take refuge in the Dharma. Dharma, or *fa* in Chinese, is the amalgam of Zen Buddhist ideas, expressions, principles, methods, and lifestyle. The Dharma, like the Buddha, has existed for all eternity across time and space. The historic Buddha recognized this amalgam during his enlightenment. He, like other historic Buddhas before him, organized them in an easily understandable teaching and carried them to his followers.

Zen Body: The Shaolin Temple of Song Mountain is placed on an ancient sacred site that has been visited by Chinese rulers for centuries. The seclusion and cultural importance of this, or any temple setting, made it easy to establish an environment to practice the Dharma. That having been said, Ta-Mo believed that each of us carries our own temple and Dharma with us everywhere we go. The occasions for sudden awakening exist everywhere and the conditions for awakening are always available.

Zen Hand: Embracing any spiritual discipline worthy of the name entails encountering difficulties. Ta-Mo emphasized the practice of both seated meditation and the Eighteen Hands moving meditation. The moving meditation, which I will discuss later, was specifically designed to help the adherent avoid some of the naturally occurring pitfalls of seated meditation. As early as four generations after Ta-Mo, practitioners outside of the Patriarch's Shaolin School were beginning to de-emphasize the Eighteen Hands method. By the Time of the Sixth Chinese Patriarch, Hui-Neng, the two practices had been separated altogether, ensuring many aberrations of Ta-Mo's original method.

Zen Heart: One of those aberrations concerned the idea of purity as mentioned in the last stanza of this canto. Many Zen meditators had so focused on the concept of the pure essence of Buddha Nature that they actually became bound to it. What resulted was the notion that an individual's original essence was, somehow, a separate entity that lay beneath the turmoil and confusion of the deluded mind. Consequently, they focused on emptying their minds completely and would not allow any thought at all to be conceived, much less investigated. These practitioners, thinking that they were cultivating purity, ended up establishing a corrupted notion of a divine and pure essence, attaching to it and pursuing it as a concrete ideal. Ta-Mo's injunction in this canto is clear: "There is no self. / There is no form or shape. / There is no other. / There is no subject and no object." There are some people who believe that sitting quietly with an empty mind is a great meditative achievement, but they are mistaken. Ta-Mo had discovered that those who had "fallen into a pit of emptiness and become purity-bound" through this practice, made no progress in the Zen Way. They had actually become trussed up in a kind of spiritual materialism that resulted in poor health, antisocial attitudes, and all sorts of aberrant psychological behavior. In the original Zen founded by Ta-Mo at the Shaolin Temple in Honan Province, the moving meditation of the Eighteen Hands insured that fledgling contemplatives would avoid becoming attached to their own spiritual endeavors. This is a core belief of Zen Buddhism.

CANTO XIII

A wisdom-thread states, "The Universal Essence
    contains no sentient beings.
Thus, it is free from the impurity of selfhood."
By examining the Universal Essence, we begin to
    achieve wisdom.
To be truly wise,
You must intuitively grasp and actively understand this.
You must put your trust in it.
Then you will automatically begin to practice the
    Dharma in daily life.

Since there is no desire to possess,
The wise person is ready to physically manifest charity,
But never begrudgingly.
They are without regret and vanity.

Since they understand the nature of emptiness,
They do not become attached to form.
In this way, they enter a life that is beneficial to them.

Once they fully realize that they are indeed
    benefiting themselves,

They can help others and teach them how to glorify
the truth of awakening.
And they accomplish this without becoming
attached to form.

COMMENTARY

Zen Mind: Examining the Universal Essence is another
way of describing the act of self-examination guided by
higher intuition. Zen philosophy recognizes several levels
of both the conscious and unconscious mind that must be
examined during meditation. The important point,
however, is that the intuitive mind, or *prajna*, must be
used to move from the Bound world of the empirical
mind to the Boundless world of Buddha Nature.

Buddha Nature is also known as the True Nature or
Self Nature. Your original mind is not filled with the
preconceptions triggered by habit, memory, suffering
and sensation. It is possessed of True Nature. Not being
filled, it is empty of preconceptions and mind-stuff. It is,
therefore, free to experience everything as profoundly
new. What the Buddhists call no-mind is actually the all-
mind of direct experience. In experiential terms, a mind
filled with knowledge and preconceptions sees a ray of
sunlight, perceives it as sunlight, recognizes it as such,

and categorizes it accordingly. A true Zen adherent, on the other hand, sees nothing. Seeing nothing, when encountering a ray of sunlight, the Zen adherent becomes the sunlight.

Zen Body: Living day-to-day in a state of emptiness means to live with as few judgments as possible. Imagine experiencing everything in the world as if it were the very first time. This leads to a feeling of unity with all existence engendered, precisely, because we all share the same emptiness. Understanding the nature of emptiness naturally leads to an outpouring of love and compassion for your fellow man. A simpler way of putting it might be that we are all in this together because we are all the same being. When you realize that we all share the same Universal Essence, you come to intrinsically believe that everything you perceive is, in reality, part of yourself.

Zen Hand: As a technique, understanding the nature of emptiness entails approaching everything that you see, do, or encounter as if you have never seen, done, or encountered it before, i.e. treating every moment in space and time as a fresh, new moment.

Zen Heart: Cultivating the faculty of Direct Experience is a primary objective in Zen that can only be achieved by understanding emptiness and not attaching your bodymind to form.

CANTO XIV

The wise ones can then practice the Six Virtues
Which form the raft that will transport them to the
    other shore.
These virtues order the thought process.
But, while they are practicing
Generosity, patience, discipline, energy, meditation,
    and wisdom,
They remain detached from the outcome as a way
    to cut through delusion.
They have no idea that they are engaged in good deeds
And in this way, though completely involved,
They practice nothing.
By practicing the Dharma in this manner,
They enter the Way with the face of transcendental
    reason.

Now go forward and look directly at the mind,
Enter the Zen Way of Life and look directly at the
    face of the Buddha.

COMMENTARY

Zen Mind: The Six Virtues are explained in the "Sermon on the Ten Perfections" and form a secret Zen teaching unique to the Shaolin School. In this sermon, Ta-Mo emphasizes the idea of not becoming attached to any of the methods of Zen cultivation. This includes the practice of the Six Virtues.

Zen Body: To behave authentically is the cornerstone of Zen living. Authentic behavior is naturally occurring, spontaneous, and uncontrived behavior. It is most easily generated by creative activity performed within a limiting construct of some kind. For example, a guitarist who improvises over a jazz standard seeks to be musically creative and original within the confines of the written song. He is seeking authenticity in his musical creation. To live the Zen life is to improvise with whatever comes your way and play over the flux and flow of change.

Some envision authenticity as a reflection of complete and total freedom where no rules or boundaries exist. They are mistaken. Complete freedom will not yield the spiritual intensity necessary to produce the lasting authenticity required for Zen awakening.

Zen Hand: As a technique, Ta-Mo emphasizes the practice of nothing. His explanation in the sermon is both profound and practical. He tells us that unselfish involvement in virtuous practice, both spontaneous and free of expectation, is the Dharma. The practice of the Six Virtues, so fundamental to Ta-Mo's original Zen method, insures the student's spiritual progress.

Zen Heart: The entire Zen approach concerns itself with total liberation from all forms of bondage. The correct practice of Zen centers on the elimination of all attachments, including attachment to correct practice. The true follower of Zen simply does Zen. He has no thought of what may or may not occur due to its practice. Think of Zen practice as something absolutely essential to your very survival. At the same time, regard it as something of only minor importance. If you can successfully balance those two perspectives, then you will catch a glimpse of the Zen heart.

SERMON TWO

SERMON ON THE
TEN PERFECTIONS

CANTO I

Hear me!
These are words that bind time, itself.
These are words that flow from the Buddha Mind.
I have heard them and, now, so shall you.
Hear them!

COMMENTARY

Zen Mind: This canto is the opening verse that is most often delivered before the recitation of Ta-Mo's sermons. From time to time, an alternate opening canto is used:

> Hear me!
> This is a secret transmission
> That takes place outside of the
>   scriptures.
> It does not depend upon words or
>   letters.

> Instead
> It points directly at your soul
> The soul of man.
>
> Hear me!
> See into your own nature
> And attain Buddhahood.

This phrase, often attributed to Ta-Mo, summarizes his entire spiritual message.

Zen Body: As a rule, followers of Zen do not concern themselves with objective validity regarding the authorship of Ta-Mo's sermons. It is important to remember, authentic Zen is an oral tradition in which at least a certain number of adherents are required to memorize the verse so as to pass it down to the next generation of followers. As these poems pass through the central nervous systems and personalities of the chosen carriers, they are frequently reshaped and subtly changed. Each generation of monks sees this as a foregone conclusion of oral circulation. As a result, Zen tradition relies on its spiritual methods to insure that Ta-Mo's authentic message is not obscured.

Zen Hand: The Zen oral and aural tradition supports Zen's spoken and, most importantly, unspoken teaching techniques. There is a rich body of method, wisdom, and lore in original Zen that has evolved into something of a spiritual folk art. The folk process often results in the evolution of historic reality to a point of concurrence with the oral tradition. Said another way, the stories that Zen monks tell one another and the manner of the telling greatly affect the practice of their meditation. However, the actual technique of Zen meditation, itself, is the most important thing. History is, oftentimes, frequently and knowingly bent as a way of intensifying the spiritual experience of a student and as a means of accelerating that student's progress toward awakening.

Zen Heart: The Zen path is, by definition, a mystical one. The opening canto, as well as its alternate, share the notion of a teaching that is far beyond description and intellection. Zen is a special teaching that flows from a place existing beyond time. This place is the Buddha Mind.

While the mystical nature of Zen may be attractive to certain personalities, it should be noted that Zen is profoundly empirical, as well. Ta-Mo, like the historic Buddha before him, encouraged his students not to accept his claims on faith. Rather, he insisted that they put his words to the test in the laboratories of their own bodyminds. Simply, trust in the good sense of the message and see for yourself. During this personal research, Cultivators of the Zen path do not attribute objective validity to anything that they may—or may not—encounter. The rational mind can always be engaged later. The mystical experience is the vital key and rationality, if engaged too soon, can prevent anything truly interesting from taking place.

CANTO II

I will speak to you now
On the six virtues and the four skills
That are sometimes called
The Ten Perfections.

The Ten Perfections form the mortar and stone of
    the monastic order that is called Shaolin-ssu.
They are literally the transcendental steps.
They are virtuous books.
They are skills developed by each and every Bodhisattva
Through the course of their training.
To the Bodhisattva,
The awakening being,
These books become a raft that reaches the other shore.
That is how we say it.

COMMENTARY

Zen Mind: The Ten Perfections are the tools employed by Zen Cultivators to bring others to awakening. But they are also the result of Zen cultivation. The canto is plain when it says that these virtues and skills manifest naturally in the Cultivator as a result of successful Zen work. Once manifested, they dramatically change the Cultivator's perspective. This perspective, strange and unfamiliar at first, must be studied and researched as one might study a book. A book, in this case, is archaic Chinese language that signifies a body of knowledge and skill. It can exist as an actual written text but most often takes the form of skill sets that are passed down in units from teacher to student.

Zen Body: The Shaolin Temple, located on Song Mountain in Honan Province, has a long established history as one of China's most important sacred sites. It is China's foremost Buddhist temple. Shaolin (*Shorin* in Japanese) means Young Forest. The temple was built around 480 C.E. by the Emperor Shao-Wen for one of Ta-Mo's predecessors named Pa-T'wo. To this day, it is home to Buddhist monks studying the Chinese Zen Way.

Zen Hand: Oral tradition holds that the Ten Perfections were an integral part of the Founders' teaching. Unfortunately, some commentators in Zen history have referred to the Perfections as "occult powers" that distract monks from the true path. As a result, even mentioning them has, from time to time, been forbidden. However, within the direct transmission of the Shaolin School, the Ten Perfections are held in high regard tempered by the belief that authentic practice will, ultimately, protect the Cultivator from diversion. The importance of a qualified Master in this process cannot be overstated.

Zen Heart: The Ten Perfections are the tools of the Bodhisattva. They are also verification of deep accomplishment in Zen. However, they are never desired or coveted, nor do they manifest completely in every Cultivator. How and to what degree they make their appearance depends upon the Karma, gifts, and deficits of the particular Zen student. The Bodhisattva is an "awakening" being and not necessarily one that has reached the fullness of enlightenment. Consequently, the six virtues and four skills manifest at different rates and in varying degrees. It is a Zen core belief that any given perfection will appear as needed and as guided by the Buddha Mind.

CANTO III

The Ten Perfections are swords
That cut through the illusions of selfness.
They slay the differentiating mind.
They save the deluded.
These perfections help us realize the Tao essence
And clearly see
The sameness of our own essential nature—
The essential nature of all living things.
I must say this forcefully: We are not separate.
We all share the same life force.

COMMENTARY

Zen Mind: The notion of the inseparability of humanity
is a vital part of the Zen mindset. Whatever, we do—no
matter how insignificant we believe it to be—affects
each and every person on the planet. The life force, or
qi, is the key to this universal connection. Everything has

qi. People, animals, trees, rocks, and soil all possess some quantity of life-force energy. We, also, live in a vast sea of *qi* that covers the planet. Our mental and physical activity causes *qi* to move both inside and outside the bodymind. The thought of hammering a nail, for example, begins to broadcast ripples of *qi* energy to the world around us even before we raise the hammer. Likewise, all of the activity that takes place in the world sends out ripples of *qi* energy that, eventually, touches each of us.

Zen Body: Ta-Mo was a member of the *ksatreya*, or Warrior class, in his native India. These individuals dedicated their martial and societal activities to higher spiritual goals even in times of relative peace. This included a highly developed moral code and ethical standard that profoundly influenced the development of Zen. Ta-Mo instilled military discipline into the daily activities of the monks at the Shaolin Temple.

Zen Hand: Discipline in your daily activities leads to discipline in your spiritual practice. This discipline is essential for any sort of Zen achievement.

Zen Heart: A Zen Cultivator lives his life as a spiritual warrior. Ta-Mo used terms like "slay," "cut," and "save" to describe the kind of interaction you must have when dealing with illusion. The sword itself in Chinese culture symbolizes unity of purpose and clarity of mind. It also symbolizes the purity of perfecting oneself for the good of all. The Ten Perfections are the weapons of the Zen warrior.

CANTO IV

Of these Ten Perfections, all are skills.
Of these Ten Perfections, all are virtues.
Of these Ten Perfections, all are steps along the path.

All of these Ten Perfections
Form the finger that points directly to the mind.

Beyond this mind, there is no Buddha.
You cannot find it.
This mind is the Buddha.

You must believe in the intelligence of this message.

Buddhists are not faithful.
This is not faith, because you will reveal it to yourself.
It is merely the truth of good sense.

The raft of which I speak does not exist in space or time.
It cannot be grasped or coveted.
It should not be grasped or coveted.
It can only be directly experienced
As a result and function of seeing
Your essential nature.

COMMENTARY

Zen Mind: This canto emphasizes the varied nature of the Ten Perfections, as well as the reason for their inclusion in the Zen Way. Specifically, they are ways of pointing directly to the mind. Each is a key with the ability to unlock the Buddha Mind.

Zen Body: The term Zen has several meanings. Meditation, in general, and the meditation technique of Ta-Mo, in specific, are only two of the accepted meanings. Zen also refers to enlightenment, cosmic reality, or catching a brief glimpse of cosmic reality. Even though Zen Buddhism aims at sudden awakening, enlightenment most often comes in incremental steps during one's lifetime.

Zen Hand: Zen is a mystical process that emphasizes direct experience. While a single mystical event can be profoundly life changing, the Zen ideal is to engineer a continuous revelation of the Boundless in the midst of the Bound. To directly experience life and bask in its glow is to embrace the technique of Zen as a practical matter. Revealing it to yourself, as stated in the canto, is an experiential process that engages various altered states of consciousness that initiate, generate, and support direct experience.

Zen Heart: The "raft that reaches the other shore" is a metaphor for the ground of being that results from Zen practice and the manifestation of the Ten Perfections. It is a fundamental Zen idea that these virtues exist outside of space and time as an extension of the Buddha Mind.

CANTO V

As I have said to you before,
If you do not find a true teacher as soon as possible,
Then your life will be wasted.
While each one of us possesses the Buddha Nature,
Without the work of a true teacher,
It will never be realized.

COMMENTARY

Zen Mind: The Shaolin School emphasizes the need for a competent and inspired teacher if *tun-wu*, or sudden awakening, is to occur. In the authentic Zen tradition, the teacher and student periodically share consciousness that supports, informs, and actualizes the various Zen spiritual practices. The teacher employs a variety of largely non-verbal techniques that grant the student deep access to his or her inner self. This is a transconscious experience in which the student is gently guided by the teacher into altered states of perception. In these altered states, the profound non-ordinary wisdom of the unconscious mind is drawn out into ordinary waking consciousness. It's as if the teacher is a spiritual conductor who leads the bodymind orchestra of the student toward awakening. In this way, the true Zen teacher cultivates the heart and mind of the student while nourishing the student's Buddha Nature.

Zen Body: Those interested in ancient Chinese Zen often mistakenly imagine that it closely resembles the Zen practices of Japan. In reality, the Zen of the first Patriarch more closely resembles Tibetan Buddhist custom, appearance, and tradition. Members of the Shaolin School refer to their brand of Dharma as The Hidden or Esoteric Buddhism.

The tenets of Zen Buddhism that establish it as an "esoteric" method are secrecy and initiation, an emphasis on direct transmission, the use of detailed visualization and symbolism as an adjunct to standard meditation, the use of stylized and symbolic physical movement designed to awaken spiritual wisdom, and Shihfu veneration. The Shihfu, or Honored Teacher, is seen as the students' living link to the wisdom of Ta-Mo. In fact, the true Teacher selectively reincarnates aspects of the first Patriarch's personality as a way of serving his students. The life of a Zen Cultivator is tied to the influence of the teacher who serves as guide and protector along the Zen path.

Zen Hand: Learning Zen spiritual techniques can be, at times, problematic. The necessity of having a teacher who "has gone before you" is important to keeping the mystical experience on track. A true teacher is one who can provide well-placed glimpses of the Tao and engineer small awakenings within the student. He also has the ability to recognize impediments to a student's practice and can intervene before they cause difficulty.

Zen Heart: The canto is clear regarding the importance of the teacher. That having been said, in the absence of a teacher or a temple setting, you can still make progress along the Zen path. Fundamentally, all that is required is the sincere devotion to turning your mind around to view itself. Then, locked in the moment of directly experiencing your own mind, you will glimpse your essential nature.

CANTO VI

THE PERFECTION OF GENEROSITY

The first Perfection is the practice of Generosity.

What does it mean to practice generosity?

True charity is the perfection of helping all sentient
   beings.
This is not to be interpreted as giving only in a
   material sense.
The beneficence must be of a spiritual nature as well.
It must pervade the three worlds
That encompass the totality of our existence.

COMMENTARY

Zen Mind: True charity, in a Zen sense, implies an
intimate contact with all beings in the three worlds of
man, earth, and heaven. This connection must be

honored. Zen Cultivators know that the development of a compassionate, giving, and amiable character is, however, only a preliminary step. A personal disposition grounded in true Zen charity leads to a merging with the cosmos and, eventually, an awareness of our own essential nature.

Zen Body: Any normal and everyday thought or action can become a charitable one. All that is required is the realization that the entirety of human activity across time and space is interconnected. True charity nullifies the disorganized energy of past bad acts and transmutes it into a momentum for good. Charitable works purify the consciousness of the world in the same way that formal Zen purifies the consciousness of the meditator.

Zen Hand: Helping other beings is a specific Zen spiritual technique. On the other hand, the solo practice of seated Zen meditation will spiritually benefit all other beings. As you cultivate yourself in meditation, the *qi* within you is condensed, shaped, and organized. As the life force within you becomes increasingly more organized, it begins to shape and arrange the *qi* immediately around you. Internal clarity generates external clarity. Eventually, waves of condensed and highly organized *qi* are transmitted outward beyond your immediate environment. Any beings that come in contact with this expanding field of organized energy will, themselves, experience the salubrious effects of your solo meditation.

Zen Heart: The Zen Way is often described as being a path that is transmitted mind to mind. But Zen Cultivators know that it is transmitted "heart to heart," as well. There is no separation between the two. I use the neologism "heartmind" to more accurately describe this fundamental Zen concept. Any perceived notion of division or separation is a product of the deluded heartmind. Cultivators intrinsically know that there is no inside or outside, no self or other. During the practice of true charity, whatever love or beneficence you extend to one heartmind, you extend to all, including your own.

CANTO VII

This pervasiveness
Must be kind and compassionate
Above all.

The practice of generosity is fully realized
By using your skills to help others.
In fact, dedicate any merit or ability or talent that you
    have
To the full awakening of all beings.

To keep these gifts to yourself
Is an abasement of the Zen Way of Life
And is a result
Of anger, greed, and delusions born of sensations.

Generosity is the hollowness of the reed.
Generosity is the emptiness of the boat
That allows it to float on the water's surface between the
    two shores.
Reading sutras and
Calling upon the Buddha's name
Will not help you.
It will not serve as a substitute for this Dharma.

COMMENTARY

Zen Mind: Chinese Zen sees no distinction between "heart," "mind," and "intention." In this case, they function together as a heartfelt desire. At all times, mentally broadcast a sincere wish for the salvation of all beings. With practice, maintaining a mental outlook of extending compassion becomes second nature. While the performance of charitable and compassionate acts is very important, the strong intent to continuously extend love and service to others profoundly nourishes the bodymind of a Zen Cultivator.

Zen Body: Dedicating your energy and skills to the awakening of all beings is simple and within the reach of every Zen Cultivator. The task chosen, however, is important. Any activity that you are good at, or in which you can become easily involved, is the kind of activity you should choose. Tasks of this kind are filled with intent. Perhaps you mow the lawn with great care and efficiency. House painting, for example, might bring you pleasure. Before beginning, say to yourself, "As I paint this house, I'll pretend that each brushstroke brushes away delusion from the mind of every person in my town." Then, proceed to paint the house while

firmly believing that you are accomplishing your
spiritual goal.

Zen Hand: Dedicating your talents to the world's
awakening is a specific Zen technique. For example, let's
say that you have musical talent. Ritualize your approach
to practice and performance as if it were a formal
contemplative activity. Be continuously mindful of the
notion that each and every note should be played or sung
with love and compassion. Be completely satisfied with
whatever you create. After all, you are playing for the
sake of others. Upon the wave of your song floats your
wish for all to see their true essence and Buddha Nature.

Zen Heart: If you have a special gift or talent and
keep it to yourself, then you create negative Karma. The
energy that manifests as individual talents and gifts is
part of the Buddha Mind and, as such, exists
everywhere. From a Zen Buddhists' perspective, talents
and gifts are the property of everyone. It is due to the
function of the demands of Karma that they are more
accessible to some than to others. Sharing your
individual gifts with other people is a way to honor the
Buddha Nature in each of us.

CANTO VIII

Before you use the name of the Buddha,
The Awakened One,
The Awakened One must be in your mind.
You must behold it
Or the words that you speak will be meaningless.
Behold your mind
And help others to nurture their waking nature,
Their Buddha Nature.
Do so without thought of return.
That is what we mean by practicing generosity.

COMMENTARY

Zen Mind: The precise intermingling of will, thought, imagination, and physical activity is vitally important to the Zen mindset. The notion that using the word "Buddha" would be of any value without the experience of what it represents is, from a Zen perspective, putting the cart before the horse. Words and their use have consequences. They affect the speaker as much, if not more, than those who hear or read the words. It's as if each word has a spirit that is intimately linked to what it represents. Your mental perspective can either honor or dishonor the spiritual connection.

Zen Body: Honoring the connection between words and what they are intimately linked to informs many aspects of Zen life. However, religious observance as a matter of form or habit should be assiduously avoided. As such, spending long hours repeating sutras and treatises on Buddhist philosophy and dogma, known as *shastra*, is meaningless. Your time would be better spent either in meditation or, more importantly, in extending kindness and compassion to others.

Zen Hand: Ta-Mo was a strict sectarian who aroused the enmity of his fellow Buddhists in India. His goal to adhere to the strict letter of the Buddha's original message became unpopular among those who were given to spiritual materialism and the formalities of worship. As a matter of Zen practice, do not look for the Buddha in temples, holy books, or elaborate ceremonies. Instead, look to your own heartmind. It is the only place where you will find the Awakened One.

Zen Heart: On his deathbed, the historic Buddha forbade both the building of statues in his honor or the offering of any devotion whatsoever in his name. He emphasized the necessity of direct human transmission of the Dharma and eschewed written texts of any kind. His wishes were honored for almost five hundred years. After that, statues and other Buddhist icons began appearing. The Buddhist canon grew in size and complexity, until the faithful spent more time making written copies of it than meditating or memorizing the few profound and plain words spoken by the Buddha. Zen emphasizes a rededication to the Buddha's original message and places little to no reliance on either the study of written texts or invocations of the Buddha's name.

CANTO IX

THE PERFECTION OF PATIENCE

The second Perfection is the practice of Patience.

What does it mean to practice patience?

At the core of this perfection
Is the skill of intuitive insight
Into the life of all sentient beings,
Including yourself.

COMMENTARY

Zen Mind: Zen places great reliance upon the intuition and prizes it far and above logical reasoning. It sits at the core of Zen. The importance of acquiring the skill of intuitive insight becomes apparent in another verse describing an event in the Buddha's life. This verse, which is not attributed to Ta-Mo, is preserved in the Zen oral tradition:

Hear me!
This is the verse of
Thought transmitted by the Thought
Without words
Neither written
Nor spoken.

The Awakened One was teaching
On the Peak of Vultures, when
The great teacher Kashpaya appeared
Presenting Him
With a golden flower
And beseeched the Awakened One
To reveal the ultimate law and doctrine.

The Awakened One held aloft
The heavenly flower
But said no word
And
Beheld the flower
In silence.

Those assembled were perplexed
But, only Kashpaya smiled
As the Awakened One spoke.
"I have formed a wonderful and clear thought
Of flower bliss and *nirvana*.
I see the center of it
In silence.
I see the eye of the ultimate law and doctrine.

I will send it to you
Kashpaya
In silence."

The Awakened One looked at
Kashpaya
And smiled.
At that moment,
Kashpaya's intuitive mind was opened
By thought
And
By thought alone.
The ultimate law was reflected
In his soul.

Kashpaya would intuitively transmit it
To Ananda.
Ananda would intuitively transmit it
To Shanavasin.
From patriarch to patriarch
Unto Ta-Mo himself,
The secret of the golden flower
Has been revealed
Mind to Mind.
From that day forward
The doctrine of the Awakened One
Has been transmitted intuitively
By thought
And thought
Alone.

Zen Body: The Zen ideal of intuitive insight parallels the Taoist concept of talking with your soul, or *shen-ling*, via the intuition. Your intuition is the voice of your soul guiding you through life. It speaks in the language of imaginings, emotions, sensations, and feelings. Living intuitively requires openness to the soul's language, as well as new ideas and concepts that challenge preconceptions and behavioral habits. Structure often becomes important when living intuitively because total freedom without limits of some kind invariably leads to a blocking of the intuition altogether.

In daily practice, the Zen Cultivator attempts to approach an ordinary and familiar task with a fresh outlook. Then, attempting to listen to the inner voice, the Cultivator proceeds with the task pretending to be amazed and intrigued by what is unfolding. He takes note of any thoughts or sensations that arise in his bodymind. To put it simply, he allows the soul to come forward and take the lead in performing the task. Distractions naturally arise. Gently, he returns to the activity allowing his intuition to guide him. The goal is to engineer a state of maximum engagement with the activity. Eventually, the Cultivator becomes truly astonished by the deep and profound connection with whatever is at hand. Life becomes a great work of art to the Zen Cultivator in which every second of involvement radically changes the body, the mind, and the spirit.

Zen Hand: Activities that boost intuition, such as calligraphy, painting, martial arts, and music, become more than mere diversions to a Zen Cultivator. They become models of how we should experience each other. We should approach each other like art.

The skill of engaging intuitive insight into the lives of all beings begins by inviting non-ordinary sense impressions into your bodymind. Every meeting should become a transcendental experience. Wisdom and mental pictures should flow into you from previously unknown quarters. Essentially, you strive to experience an individual in the same way that you might experience the performance of a Bach prelude or Beethoven symphony. Try to "listen" with your heart and soul to everyone that you meet. Begin by giving them your complete and undivided attention. Then, without judgment, observe your own thoughts and sense impressions. What comes to mind when you meet this person or that? Do they trigger any sensations in your bodymind or any memories from your past? Do not attribute objective validity to anything you sense. Instead, merely observe events as if you were a mirror reflecting everything and missing nothing.

Allowing the life force and personality of an individual to flow into you like music will begin to train the Zen skill of *prajna*, or intuitive insight. Soon, you will gain great wisdom and insight into your own life and the lives of those around you. The key, of course, is to be patient enough to allow the experience to unfold at its own pace.

Zen Heart: The practice of engaging ever-increasing levels of mindfulness in your interactions with other people automatically leads to more openness and receptivity. Soon, your intuition will begin to speak to you with more vividness and clarity. With that clarity comes the promise of something more than mere habitual and judgmental reaction. Indeed, something far more wondrous becomes possible. Boundless patience for your fellow man manifests, and human interaction, guided by your intuition, literally becomes nourishment. Then, as a Cultivator of the Zen Way, you will feed on life itself.

CANTO X

Who in this world does not have difficulty and problems?
Those who are searching for the Tao path
Will always encounter adversity,
But in perfecting patience,
They must not be steered away from seeking their
    essential nature,
For that is the most important work.

COMMENTARY

Zen Mind: Encountering difficulty when practicing the Zen Way is a foregone conclusion. In fact, if a student isn't experiencing difficulty in either formal or informal practice, then it is the duty of the master to provide some. To detach emotionally from problems while blissfully telling yourself that "all is well" is not true Zen.

Zen Body: Every problem or difficulty that comes up during Zen practice should be regarded as an opportunity to catch a glimpse of your essential nature. As a practical matter, how each of us confronts and handles problems is a reflection of our moral character. Think of a problem as a gift from the Tao and look into it intuitively. Do not respond to it as you normally would. Try to see it in a new perspective. Examine it with your intuition and allow clues to its resolution to bubble up from deep within you.

Zen Hand: Although Zen emphasizes sudden awakening, the process of orchestrating the *tun-wu* can be very frustrating for the Cultivator. It is a very subtle affair that can be easily derailed, and placing too much importance on difficulties encountered along the way is the surest way to derail it. Accepting physical, mental, or emotional discomfort during meditation, for example, should be viewed merely as mysteries of the Zen process. Take note of each, as you would any distraction, and move past them.

Zen Heart: First and foremost, having true Zen patience is having patience with one's self. Frequently, people are very patient with others but have difficulty extending that same patience to themselves. If you do not have the willingness to endure your own shortcomings, then any patience or tolerance extended to others will be of no use whatsoever. Simply put, being patient with yourself is more important than being patient with others.

CANTO XI

Be tolerant
Of the temperament and aggression of others.
Always remember that these problems have a cause.

Use your intuition to look at these disturbances and,
Without judgment,
Let the causal factors speak directly to you.

Use this same insight to be patient with yourself
And realize that correctness is a dynamic state
That is very difficult to describe.

There is no self or other ultimately,
No right and wrong ultimately;
You can only be essentially correct at any point in
    time and space.
All things are part of a cycle.
They are constantly in motion.

The shape of this patience,
The shape of this perfection,
Is like the shape of a boat that fits perfectly in any
    body of water.

That is how the Shaolin monks say "freedom."

COMMENTARY

Zen Mind: It is only natural for Zen Cultivators to be concerned with progress. However, your progress cannot be discussed in terms of "good or bad" or "right and wrong." At any given moment, your practice can only be "essentially correct" to a greater or lesser degree. It's as if you embark on a journey from coast to coast. A straight route would be preferable, but things come up that alter your direct course. Though detours occur, you keep your original goal in mind and gently correct your course as need be. Along the way, you enjoy the sites presented by the detours. Eventually, you arrive at your destination or, more often, somewhere close to it. The journey, one of self-discovery, is the most important thing. The destination becomes secondary.

From a Zen perspective, the quality of life, formal practice, informal practice, and human interaction cannot be judged in an accurate and qualitative way because it is constantly moving and shifting as a result of Karma. You can only trust that you are essentially correct; that you are generally moving in the right direction.

Zen Body: Being tolerant of the temperament and aggression of others does not mean that you should ever allow yourself to become a victim of their behavior. Defense of one's life and wellness is not only an acceptable course but a Zen mandate as well. Even the Buddha himself frequently traveled the wild countryside of India with an entourage of warrior protectors.

Modern Buddhism too often takes a passive role when confronting violence and aggression. That having been said, examples from the ancient period do exist. Zen oral tradition recounts tales of the total destruction of Indian Buddhism by the warriors of Allah, circa 1200 C.E. The destruction of Buddhism in the land of its birth is attributed, in large part, to a degeneration of the original intent and meaning of the historic Buddha's message. The moral of these tales revolves around the notion that a philosophy that becomes inflexible and overly complex will be unable to survive. Buddhist pacifism as we know it in a modern context is, historically, something of a recent development and more closely associated with the Hinayana philosophy of detachment from the world. The Zen Buddhism of Ta-Mo, on the other hand, reflects a willingness to engage aggression and evil as it presents itself with an eye to its speedy resolution even if resolution involves meeting evil with a closed fist. At best, Zen aims to intuitively investigate aggression as it occurs while seeking ways to requite it and prevent future aggression. This proactive stance makes it easier to tolerate the aberrant behavior of others. Intuitive insight into the roots of aggressive behavior also helps in devising specific strategies for preempting future violence.

It is important to remember that Ta-Mo, not unlike the Buddha, came from a warrior tradition. Likewise, the Chinese culture of the time had its own warrior ethic. This ethic greatly influenced the moral and ethical code of the Chinese people as well as the Buddhist monks of Shaolin. The location of the Shaolin Temple was itself a sacred site routinely visited by generals and great warriors. These individuals recognized the importance of the skilled warrior in society. The act of dedicating martial skill to both the overall betterment of society and to higher spiritual goals was a routine facet of Chinese life. Along those lines, dedicating oneself to the spiritual salvation of every sentient being in the world virtually requires the strength, focus, and fortitude of a great warrior. It is this frame of mind that must be brought to the Zen practice of patience so as to inform day-to-day behavior.

Zen Hand: Accurately judging the quality of Zen practice is best left to a qualified Zen Master. That having been said, the indications of essentially correct Zen practice are:

- Elevated levels of peace, relaxation, and freshness.
- Heightened sensory alertness with a greater appreciation for the beauty of life and the wonders of nature.

- Physical and emotional stability.
- Enhanced mental focus and concentration.
- Greater physical strength and enhanced communication skills.
- Elevated levels of compassion and caring for others.
- An awareness of something much greater than yourself.
- A willingness to fearlessly meet life squarely as it comes.
- An overwhelming sense of cheerfulness and a positive mental attitude.
- Being astonished by the depth and clarity of your thinking.

Zen Heart: The Zen concept of "no right and wrong" has nothing to do with morality. Rather, it is self-referential with regards to progress along the Zen path. At no point in your cultivation will you experience a breakthrough and arrive at some exalted "right" place. Awakening is not an arrival point. It is only the beginning of your journey. To be essentially correct, as opposed to either right or wrong, honors the changing nature of the Tao. It also honors the notion that someone who is not yet awakened simply cannot, with certainty, know anything.

CANTO XII

THE PERFECTION OF DISCIPLINE

The third Perfection is the practice of Discipline.

What does it mean to practice discipline?

To follow the Dharma path of discipline
Is to conduct yourself in accord with morality.
Be tolerant of others and treat them with kindness and
    charity.
This is the morality of your essential nature.

It is a profound initiation.
It will ensure the elimination of rampant passions.
It is a prerequisite of Zen training.

COMMENTARY

Zen Mind: Discipline, from a Zen perspective, is a
balanced approach to spiritual involvement. That is,

doing good for yourself and for others in equal amounts. It requires great focus to see the suffering in the world and not sacrifice yourself completely to eradicating it. The reality is that you must be fully alive, engaged, and at your best to effectively help others.

Zen Body: The Zen moral code is outlined and exemplified in the Ten Perfections. They are an extension of the Six Paramitas of Mahayana Buddhism, which are the practices of charity, kindness, tolerance, perseverance in Buddhist practice, meditation that leads to mystic experience, and the cultivation of intuitive wisdom.

Zen Hand: This entire sermon serves as a guide to Zen practice. As a kind of spiritual shorthand, Zen adherents will say that three of the paramitas (charity, kindness, and tolerance) are for the benefit of others, while the remaining three (perseverance, mystic meditation, and intuitive wisdom) benefit Cultivators. Fundamentally, they know that all six inform and support each other, creating an overlapping matrix that elevates the Buddha Nature in everyone.

Zen Heart: Kindness, moral behavior, charity, tolerance, and the positive effects of Zen practice are all fundamental parts of your essential nature. Said another way, it is your basic nature to be calm, happy, alert, tolerant, giving, relaxed, focused, strong, and astonished by life. This is your authentic birthright. Unfortunately, illusion has gotten in the way. Through Zen practice you begin to reclaim your essential self amid the rampant confusion created by your false life.

CANTO XIII

We call it the Dharma of no excess,
The Dharma of balance and
The Dharma of non-injury.
With this Dharma you will requite any extreme
When dealing with sentient beings.
Discipline cuts through the delusions
That lead to the injuring of others
And the injuring of the self.
It is like the prow of a boat
That cuts through the surface of the water
And makes the journey a reality.

COMMENTARY

Zen Mind: The Dharma of discipline can best be understood as bringing elevated levels of balance, poise, and equilibrium to all phases of life. Requiting is the act of balancing out and reconciling. To put it simply, a Zen Cultivator seeks to fully align his behavior with his values as a means of striking a balance between thought and action. For example, we may feel grateful in our hearts and think that we carry this sense of gratitude in our minds, as well. However, if we do not behave in a grateful manner, then the gratitude is inauthentic. To spontaneously behave in an uncontrived manner that is consistent with our values reflects a bodymind seeking a disciplined state of ease and balance.

Zen Body: Our bodies must be intrinsically aligned with our psyches to perfect the practice of discipline. From a practical perspective, a lifestyle that is too cerebral lacks the balance of physicality. Say, for example, that you spend four hours reading a book. Zen would remind you that an equal amount of time should be spent in some kind of physical activity. To be sure, formulae of this kind are a bit artificial, but the point should be well taken. A life that relies heavily on one kind of endeavor, be it mental, physical, spiritual, fanciful, or practical, is a life out of balance. Being out of balance results in injury that affects the individual as well as his community. In fact, from a Buddhist perspective, self-injury is automatically injury to the entire world.

Zen Hand: The practice of the Eighteen Hands, for example, is specifically designed to balance out the time a Zen Cultivator spends in seated meditation. In fact, the entire art of Shaolin Kung-Fu is designed to be an adjunct to advanced seated meditation. In the absence of qualified instruction in Shaolin Kung-Fu, also known as *ch'uan-fa*, almost any physical activity will suffice as long as it is approached in a Zen Way. Most modern fitness activities are not suitable. *Tai chi* and *qigong* would be the best choice, followed by the practice of *yoga* and, with modification, other martial arts. Walking, swimming, and light manual labor, all approached as contemplation, will yield satisfactory results as long as the mental, emotional, and spiritual goals are aligned with the physical activity.

Zen Heart: The Zen idea of dynamic balance as a foundation for discipline extends even to spiritual attainment. A Judeo-Christian perspective, exemplified by the Desert Fathers of early Christianity, might emphasize a total dedication to the spiritual that takes the form of a dramatic renunciation of the phenomenal world and complete removal from it. This is not the Zen Way. The Buddhism of Ta-Mo requires contact with the outside world so that it can be directly influenced by the energy of Zen. In this way, Zen is often called the teaching that extends from the single heart of the initiated to the many hearts of the uninitiated.

CANTO XIV

THE PERFECTION OF DEVOTION AND ENERGY

The fourth Perfection is the practice of Devotion and
    Energy.

What does it mean to practice devotion and energy?

Here at the Temple of the Young Forest,
We speak a great deal of the nature of spiritual exertion.

Simply put,
To perfect the virtue of energy
Is to delve into the very nature of effort
And using that effort to view the Buddha Mind.

COMMENTARY

Zen Mind: Perfecting the virtue of energy entails
engineering a direct experience of your own habitual

patterns of thought and action. The totality of the self, as understood by normal perception, forms the basis of these habits and preconceptions.

Zen Body: Understanding the proper use of exertion and effort is vital to successfully cultivating an authentic Zen Buddhist lifestyle. Modern approaches to Buddhism, for example, often place great emphasis on picking just the right time and place for meditation. Too great an emphasis on the meditative environment, such as a beautiful and peaceful setting, reduces Zen to a diversion. If you only sat in formal practice when it felt comfortable, convenient and "just right," eventually, you wouldn't sit at all. Likewise, stopping a Zen meditative session because of physical or emotional discomfort, all too often, means stopping short of achieving any real progress. Knowing the importance of regular sessions, as well as when to extend effort in order to push through discomfort and when not to, is part of understanding the nature of exertion.

Zen Hand: The Eighteen Hands of Ta-Mo are spiritual exercises in the fashion of the Christian spiritual exercises of St. Ignatius. Each aims at achieving a deeper spirituality. The Eighteen Hands spiritually shape the Zen Cultivator. They renew the Cultivator's dedication and enthusiasm, while providing guidance on the proper use of mental, physical, and spiritual force.

Zen Heart: Understanding the interplay of the forces that make up authentic Zen devotion and energy eventually leads to a profound understanding of *tzu-jan*, or spontaneity and naturalness. Only in the light of this authenticity can we transcend mental discrimination and glimpse the Tathagata-womb in each of us.

CANTO XV

There is no Buddha outside of the mind.
There is no effort outside the mind.

Devout, clear, and unrelenting effort
Is the only way to behold the mind.
True exertion is a deeply transforming feeling
That is not affected by alien forces.
This is the character of the Zen Way.
You must learn to use this character,
This special energy,
To transmute the gross, or the large,
To the fine, or small.
This task requires great devotion.
To refine the large to the small is our task.

COMMENTARY

Zen Mind: Transmuting the large to the small entails altering the perception and consciousness in order to rearrange our habitual patterns of thought and action. This is, essentially, a purposeful confrontation of our own self-centeredness.

Zen Body: To live in a bodymind that constantly challenges its own self-centeredness requires great focus and discipline. More importantly, however, it requires a pervasive sense of humor and the ability to laugh at one's own shortcomings. Approached with a sense of humor, the act of seeking to behold the mind becomes a great adventure driven by astonishment and the pure wonder of a child exploring his world for the first time.

Zen Hand: Having reorganized a preconceived notion or habitual pattern of thought or behavior, the Zen Cultivator mystically re-experiences it. The Eighteen Hands are specifically designed to facilitate this re-experiencing process.

Zen Heart: In reality, complex illusions and ingrained preconceptions are merely small assumptions stacked one on top of another. These assumptions, however, are arranged in imposing and menacing constructs. They stand between us, and a complete experience of our lives. They effectively block our path to awakening. It is the mystic character of the Zen Way to bathe these impediments to authentic living in the light of clear awareness. The Zen light of clear awareness reduces these illusions to their constituent parts and dissolves them, altogether.

CANTO XVI

Be involved
With the energy, the effort, and the devotion
Of the Eighteen Hands,
And you will learn to wake up
And point directly to the mind.
This energy is one of the energies of awakening.
This energy will awaken you and keep you awake,
Make no mistake.

The energy, effort, and devotion
Of the Eighteen Hands
Are like the winds that fill the sail of the boat
On its journey to the other side.

COMMENTARY

Zen Mind: Words are not necessary for the
communication of Zen. In fact, words as fossilized
poems frequently retard our understanding of the ideas

they intend to communicate. It is a basic Zen concept that the body does not move; only the mind moves. Physical movements of the hands and arms are, in reality, movements of the mind. Dedicated involvement in the apparently physical practice of the Eighteen Hands of Ta-Mo gradually reveals the inner workings of the mind.

Zen Body: A Zen life rides on a self-generated cushion of spiritual energy. We must make an effort, accumulate time spent in our efforts, and maintain a spirit of exploration along the way. Since we move through and explore the so-called outer world with our arms and legs, it seems only natural to explore our inner world in the same way. The energy of cultivating a physical Zen, as it were, brings us closer to a cultivation of mental Zen.

Zen Hand: The Eighteen Hands, which I will examine in the "Sermon on Mind-to-Mind Transmission," are specially designed as transformative movement and physical meditation. They support the Zen concept of intuitive insight and the wordless search for the original mind. Because of an intimate connection to the inner workings of the mind, Ta-Mo's Eighteen Hands provide both the clues and the motive force for their investigation.

Awakening, whether sudden or gradual, is a delicate thing. Zen Cultivators, post awakening, can find themselves becoming, once again, mired in illusion. The spiritual energy, effort, and devotion generated by the practice of the Eighteen Hands will help prevent this regression.

CANTO XVII

THE PERFECTION OF MEDITATION

The fifth Perfection is the practice of Meditation.

What does it mean to practice the virtue of meditation?

The Buddha had but one message,
And that is the message of meditation.

The art and craft of awareness
Is the method that contains all other methods.
As such, it is vast yet simple in its profundity.

COMMENTARY

Zen Mind: The Zen Buddhist mindset rests squarely on the idea of meditation as the most effective means to cut through illusion and achieve awakening. All other methods and approaches to awakening must be held to the standard of self-investigative meditation.

Zen Body: Zen aims to liberate all people, not just the devout. Even those who don't believe in the good sense of the Buddha's message or who engage in monstrous evil are worthy of salvation. Likewise, other religions and philosophies that are dedicated to compassion, kindness, and the awakening of the world are accepted as welcome companions on the path. No matter how different the methods, rituals, or approaches might be, any path that shares, in some way, the original meditative ideal of the Buddha is judged to be worthy. In that sense, the Zen Buddhist lives a life that contains all other lives and practices a religion that contains all other religions.

Zen Hand: The next canto succinctly lays out the simplest and most accessible form of Zen meditation. It is the technique by which the Buddha himself achieved awakening.

Zen Heart: The truth of meditation forms the center of the Zen Buddhist heart. Without meditation, Buddhism does not exist.

CANTO XVIII

An ancient wisdom-thread states,
"Go to a forest or the foot of a tree and sit plainly
    and simply.
While breathing out, realize it as breathing out.
While breathing in, realize it as breathing in."
This is a primal act,
And it is the best way to see your essential nature.
Illusions cannot find a foothold in this practice,
Nor can the ego become self-protective.
As a pathway to liberation, there is no method superior
Than this practice of awareness.
As you pass through the walls and mountains
With your bodymind,
You will directly experience
Joyousness, calmness, mind, mind-objects, and others.
You will rediscover yourself and see
That there is no self or other.

Shaolin is the science of mindful rediscovery.
It is this virtue that you must perfect.
It is the sail that serves the boat.

That is how we say it.

COMMENTARY

Zen Mind: Meditation must be infused with the spirit of simplicity and playfulness if it is to remain vibrant and robust.

Zen Body: This canto beautifully presents not only the doctrine of meditation, but also the idea that authentic joy and peace may be attained through a simple shift of the imagination.

Zen Hand: The instructions, however plain, serve as a reminder to the Zen Cultivator to keep his spiritual practice honed to an uncomplicated point. The awareness generated by an uncomplicated meditative practice simply will not allow much room for error.

Passing through walls and mountains is a metaphor for the dissolution of preconceptions and habitual patterns of thought and action. Oral legend speaks of Ta-Mo as the Wall-Gazing Priest who sat before a cave wall in silent meditation for nine years before realizing the profound truth of Zen.

Zen Heart: All of the knowledge and wisdom in the universe is locked away deep within each of us. Our goal, if we can be said to have one, is to search for, discover, and access that knowledge and wisdom. It should be noted that the original members of the Shaolin order residing at Song Mountain dedicated their entire spiritual life to the process of mindfully rediscovering and reinventing themselves on a daily basis. To approach every day with the spirit, clarity, and freshness of a novice became a singular feature of these Zen pioneers.

CANTO XIX

THE PERFECTION OF PERFECT WISDOM

The sixth Perfection is the practice of Perfect Wisdom.

What does it mean to practice the virtue of perfect
    wisdom?

Higher knowledge guides the boat like a rudder.
It is also the shining star that you navigate by.
Words cannot describe it;
Labels will not clarify it.

COMMENTARY

Zen Mind: Higher knowledge, in this context, is a high
level of intuitive insight that steadfastly guides the life of
the Zen Cultivator. Intuition, which normally comes in
brief flashes of awareness, flows into the bodymind in a

near continuous stream. This experience begins a process of inner clarification in which the route to our essential nature is straightened and cleared of obstructions.

Zen Body: Experiencing day-to-day life while in the throes of higher knowledge has a profound effect on those around you. Simply put, the *qi* created in the wake of the experience spills over to positively affect the body, minds, and spirits of everyone you encounter. This spiritual osmosis, resulting from existing within a high level of intuitive awareness, forms the primary act of compassion displayed by the Zen Buddhist.

Zen Hand: Progress as a practitioner of Zen is impossible without elevated levels of intuitive insight. Consequently, any activity that helps free the intuitive mind can be said to be a Zen activity.

Zen Heart: Many Zen experiences are mystical in nature and quite beyond the power of words to describe. Traditionally, artistic expression is employed as a means of surrounding the salient features of the Zen mystic experience.

CANTO XX

An ancient wisdom-thread states,
"The magic of this perfection is diminished by the
    use of words.
It can only be felt as mind."
This is difficult to understand.
It can cause much confusion to those on the path.
Seek out a true teacher to intimately transmit the learning
Of the direct wisdom of the mind.

It is pure consciousness,
A living wisdom,
Which builds to an awakening and must be sustained
    thereafter.

I will speak no more of this.
If you fixate on a thing, it vanishes.

COMMENTARY

Zen Mind: Thoughts have great power, but how we put those thoughts to action is what affects us the most. The linkage of thoughts to words and actions creates a dynamic force that profoundly influences us. The practice of perfect wisdom allows us to understand the intricacies of this process.

Zen Body: Zen Cultivators do not spend a great deal of time discussing the nature of creativity. Instead, they engage in creative pursuits as a way to actualize both the ideal and the experience of intuition.

Zen Hand: As a technique, a Buddhist guided by a continuous stream of intuition transmits rarified consciousness that purifies his home, family, and community. As this rarified consciousness reverberates to all quarters, it feeds back on the Zen Cultivator, creating even higher levels of intuitive insight.

Zen Heart: The manifestation of a continuous stream of intuitive insights forever alters the Zen Cultivator. This event remains a watershed moment in the life of a Zen Cultivator.

CANTO XXI

THE PERFECTION OF RIGHT MEANS

The seventh Perfection is practicing the skill of Right
 Means.

What does it mean to practice the skill of right means?

As you progress along the path, you will,
As guided by a true teacher,
Learn the proper methods of teaching the Absolute
In the phenomenal world.
That is, the world of attachment and illusion.

Teaching the Absolute is a means to awakening.
Teaching the Absolute is produced by awakening.

As both a product of and means to your awakening,
This skill in expounding the tenets of the Buddha Mind
Will naturally manifest.
Skillfully, you will learn to lead all sentient beings
Away from the deathlike trance that imprisons them,
And through an absurd navigation,
Help each of them reach the other shore.

Right Means will manifest with
No attachment and no discrimination.

COMMENTARY

Zen Mind: Essentially, the seventh Perfection involves a spontaneous manifestation of teaching skill. This manifestation heralds the emergence of the Bodhisattva Vow.

Zen Body: Zen Buddhists live their lives confident in the belief that every single person, place, or thing they encounter is capable of facilitating a glimpse into cosmic reality. Embracing the responsibility of teaching others vastly increases the possibility of those glimpses.

Zen Hand: The act of teaching the Dharma as a means of Zen cultivation involves an intimate partnership between student and teacher. In effect, the master and the pupil teach one another as the Buddha Dharma is educed, or drawn out, from the bodymind of the student. Such a guided eduction can take unexpected twists and turns. It takes a Zen Master who fully embraces the intuitive to successfully navigate these waters.

Zen Heart: A teacher cannot lead a student to a place where the teacher has not been. The idea of direct transmission relies heavily on the ability of each generation of Buddhist teachers to clearly recreate their own personal spiritual experience within their students. How this evolves varies greatly from student to student. The Zen Cultivator knows that each of us achieves salvation in a different way. As such, they do not become attached to any single teaching technique, preferring, instead, to work with whatever the Tao provides.

CANTO XXII

There are many beings to be led,
But none may be led by skill that is unsupported by virtue.
Make no mistake:
All that is
Can wake you
To all that is.
A sound, a word, a blow to your body, a movement,
Even a gentle breeze moving through the forest
Can point directly to the mind.

This is the first skill that you employ to reach the
    other shore.
This is the best skill that you employ to reach the
    other shore.

COMMENTARY

Zen Mind: No matter how skilled one is as a teacher,
if talent is unsupported by compassion and authentic
spiritual virtue, all will be lost.

Zen Body: The best way to cultivate compassion and spiritual virtue is to bring the mystic experience of complete union to every aspect of your life. This is especially true of your job as a teacher of the Dharma.

Zen Hand: Compassion and mystic accomplishment are the fundamental Zen spiritual experiences. They are not Zen attributes; they are the Zen Way.

Zen Heart: Under the influence of a mystic realization of life and imbued with the force of compassion, the Zen Cultivator presents himself as ripe for awakening. Almost anything can trigger it. Almost anything can sustain it. Ultimately, this is a realization of our shared humanity with all beings. At that point, compassion becomes a tender resolve and a dedicated solicitude that goes beyond the act of simply caring for others.

CANTO XXIII

As you exercise this skill,
The mind is refined and,
With staunch resolve,
You will see the *chitta*,
The "pure consciousness."

This is the perfection of Right Means.
That is how we say it.

COMMENTARY

Zen Mind: All of the knowledge, wisdom, the seeds of
every type of psychological behavior or phenomenon,
and the collective experiences of every individual life in
the universe exists in a field of pure consciousness, or
chitta. This is the basic substance that forms the essence
of the world. With practice, the Zen Cultivator begins to
dip into this vast storehouse where all things exist as
"processes of knowing." The modus operandi of

perception, in which the creative imagination produces outside objects and the external world, is seen in its' true light. The birth of a new form of ideation takes place within the Zen Cultivator, whose entire being is changed forever.

Zen Body: The life of a Zen Cultivator awash in *chitta* is a profoundly mystic existence. Everything is seen and experienced as a facet of the Ultimate Reality, or *tathata*. From the first time *chitta* is touched, the fundamental notions of learning and education are changed. With normal learning theory turned on its ear, the Cultivator viscerally participates in a brand new universe, relearning, as it were, everything he has ever learned. A new life personality emerges. The emergence of this new ground of being is a prerequisite for the spontaneous manifestation of the Bodhisattva Vow, which is the Eighth Perfection.

Zen Hand: All of the Zen techniques that prepare you for the total experience of pure consciousness can be summed up in one injunction: Endeavor to bring newness to everything that you know, have known, or ever will know.

Zen Heart: Be a beginner. No matter how much skill you possess, be a beginner. No matter how much knowledge you have, be a beginner. No matter how much capacity for helping others you have, be a beginner. Do not ignore your skills, your knowledge, or your innate capacity and pretend that they do not exist. Indeed, you must honor them. How do you honor them in the Zen Way? Be a beginner.

CANTO XXIV

The Dragon that is the thinking mind and its offspring
Will be obvious to you,
And you will naturally manifest a vow to awaken
Yourself and others
Toward liberation.
Employing Right Means leads to this vow
Which is the next perfection.

COMMENTARY

Zen Mind: The Dragon is a Zen metaphor for the
substance of the mind that gives rise to perception and
thinking. The Tiger, mentioned in the next canto, is a Zen
metaphor for the total bodymind engaged in the process
of perception and thinking. *Chitta* clearly reveals the
workings of the Dragon and the Tiger in both the
Cultivator and those he encounters.

Zen Body: The last four cantos present a profound notion: Pure consciousness is revealed as a direct result of human interaction. To elucidate, Zen meditation (the Fifth Perfection) gives rise to a continuous stream of intuition (the Sixth Perfection). The higher wisdom generated by this stream overflows "away from" personal self-centeredness and naturally generates an outflowing wave of Dharma instruction in attaining the Absolute (the Seventh Perfection). This wave flows away from the Cultivator to those around him. As the natural human give and take of learning develops, refines, and intensifies, pure consciousness is revealed. Think about that for a moment. Zen believes that human beings must work together to experience the unobstructed beauty of the universe. Furthermore, this environment of teaching and transmission is required for the total experience of *chitta*, or pure consciousness. A life informed by this perspective is forever changed.

Zen Hand: The "Sermon on the Ten Perfections" is a schematic detailing the step-by-step evolution of the authentic Zen Cultivator. Expositions of this kind are important in the Zen tradition because they insure that one does not stray from the true path. In a sense, if you know what is to occur, then you know when progress is, or is not, being made.

Zen Heart: Zen Buddhists often refer to this moment in spiritual evolution as "standing at the gates of paradise." Paradise, in this case, should not be thought of as an actual location. Rather, it is a state of consciousness that can best be described as a return to a field of innocence that is a vital part of our original essence and Buddha Nature. Walking into Eden and resting in God's hands, to use a Judeo-Christian image, takes place when the Bodhisattva Vow manifests spontaneously.

CANTO XXV

THE PERFECTION OF THE BODHISATTVA VOW

The eighth Perfection is the manifested Bodhisattva Vow.

You cannot take this vow.
It must present itself to you.
It is the Tiger subdued;
The force of a resolute mind looking at itself.
The Bodhisattva Vow will initiate you
Into the world of your essential nature.
That is how we say it.

COMMENTARY

Zen Mind: *Bodhi* means "awakened" and implies a dynamic union of boundless compassion and transcendental wisdom. *Sattva* refers to a "warrior of peace who is composed, harmonious, and upright." It also implies the natural forthrightness of a hero or heroine.

Zen Body: It is true that many Buddhists through the ages have, contrary to Ta-Mo's injunction, purposefully taken the Bodhisattva Vow. At first, this ritual practice represented a wish that the Zen initiate hoped to fulfill in his lifetime. Unfortunately, over the centuries, it became a conscious and dogmatic act. The authentic Vow is something that should take the Cultivator by surprise. It is not something that should be desired for or coveted. It happens when it happens. The true Zen Cultivator should remain mindful of the implications of being a Bodhisattva, which is, specifically, to be a servant dedicated to the awakening of all beings. Beyond that, he should spiritually expect nothing but be prepared for everything.

Zen Hand: At this point, the entire life and practice of the Cultivator supports a manifestation of the Bodhisattva Vow. From a historical perspective, other Buddhist schools have routinely devised methods of consciously working toward Bodhisattva-hood. Some of the methods are arduous and complex, requiring isolation and, often, a lifetime of ascetic practice. But the authentic Zen method revolves around the idea that becoming a Bodhisattva is a natural act of unselfish service and elegant confirmation of properly cultivating Buddha Nature.

Zen Heart: The manifestation of the Bodhisattva Vow is a spiritual introduction to a condensed field of latent *qi* that resides deep within the bodymind. It is also an initiation into the properties and uses of this energy. Once this energy begins to flow from the bodymind, it produces continuous and inexhaustible waves of positive karmic benefits that uplift the entire world.

CANTO XXVI

THE PERFECTION OF THE TEN STRENGTHS

The ninth Perfection consists of manifested skills
     called the Ten Strengths.

What does it mean to perfect the Ten Strengths?

True teaching will lead us directly to the mind
And not to another level of teaching.
Please remember that there is no goal
Outside that of recognizing the Buddha Mind
And looking upon it.

When the Bodhisattva Vow naturally manifests,
You will begin to realize and reexperience
The boundless compassion of the Buddha.
From this compassion toward all living beings
Will rise the ten powerful strengths.

These strengths are the tools of perfect wisdom
For the awakening beings of perfect wisdom.
You will become that being of perfect wisdom.

COMMENTARY

Zen Mind: Beyond viewing the mind, there is no other authentic Zen teaching. This is the spiritual goal of Zen.

Zen Body: The bodymind of the Cultivator radically changes during this phase of his training. In many cases, he must take the time to relearn even the most mundane and usual of everyday tasks. It is a period of intense spiritual reorganization that is sometimes called an "absorption."

Zen Hand: This canto places emphasis on the subduing of the bodymind engaged in the acts of perception and thinking. Zen Cultivators see this as an organizing of the various constituent parts of the bodymind. That is, meditative tasks that involve very specific physical, mental, emotional, and spiritual activity. Furthermore, these meditative activities are arranged in a programmed manner that is just as specific. The goal of each, to use a Zen phrase, "is to employ the Tiger to view the mind." All of traditional Shaolin Kung-Fu falls into this category of meditative activity.

Zen Heart: The manifestation of the Bodhisattva Vow and the latent *qi* that it releases triggers exceptional human functions that form both the spiritual powers of the Bodhisattva, as well as the tools he employs in his quest to assist his fellow beings. Zen Buddhists refer to them interchangeably as powers, strengths, and wise forces.

CANTO XXVII

COMMENTS ON EACH POWER

These are the strengths and powers.

1 The strength of perfect wisdom brings knowledge
  Of the time of ripening for the fruits of action
  And what effects it has or will have on the planter
      of that seed.

2 The power of perfect wisdom brings knowledge
  Of the myriad points of existence
  And what is possible and impossible in them.

3 The strength of perfect wisdom reveals
  The various abilities and talents of all living beings
  As well as the depth and breadth of them.

4 The power of perfect wisdom instantaneously reveals
  The proclivities of all living beings
  Within their obvious existence.

5 Likewise, the strength of perfect wisdom provides
  All knowledge
  Concerning the death and rebirth of these beings.

6 The power of perfect wisdom is like a beacon.
  It illuminates
  The diverse component parts of the world and all of its
      essence.

7 The strength of perfect wisdom shows
  The various root pathways
  That lead to the many realms of being.

8 The power of perfect wisdom grants insight
  Into
  What produces purity and what produces impurity
  In the Three Realms and the Eight Places.

9 The strength of perfect wisdom lays bare
  The dis-ease of desire,
  The dis-ease of becoming,
  The dis-ease of ignorance,
  The dis-ease of arrogance,
  And, most importantly,
  When the momentum of these defilements will deplete
      itself.
  When and where does it end?
  The man of excellent virtue will know.

10 The power of perfect wisdom bestows
  All knowledge concerning the various states of
  Contemplation,
  Concentration,
  Meditation,

Awakening, and
Absorption.

These are the ten powers of the Bodhisattva.
That is how we say it.

Note: The commentary that follows fully encompasses those elements representative of Zen Mind, Body, Hand, and Heart used in this volume.

The Ten Powers/ Strengths of the Bodhisattva

The Ten Powers of the Bodhisattva are, in essence, clairsentient abilities that allow the Bodhisattva to deeply penetrate the phenomenal world and all of the beings in it. With the knowledge gained by this investigation, the Warrior of Awakening is able to discern what each person needs in order to become fully awakened to his or her Buddha Nature.

1 The first power of the Bodhisattva is intuitive insight into the outcome of human deeds. Specifically, he is able to see what the future effects of any given action will be.

The more intent-full an action, the clearer the outcome will be to the Bodhisattva. Also, he is able to see precisely what future effects the deed will have on the person performing it.

2 The Bodhisattva is able to mystically determine what is possible or impossible in any given situation. He is able to perceive the interplay of past, present, and future events. For example, let's say a Zen monk is given a meditative task to perform. Within moments, the Zen Master will be able to "see" if anything will come from it. He then may alter the task until he knows that it will accomplish the future spiritual goal.

3 The Bodhisattva is able to look at any human talent and instantly see if it can be used to speed the Cultivator toward enlightenment. Sometimes, the Bodhisattva will discover a talent that will actually interfere with the student's progress. The student may be asked to not indulge that talents expression. The Bodhisattva can also see talent's and abilities that are latent within the student and draw them out.

4 This is profound insight into human tendencies. In short, the Bodhisattva knows how a person will react to a given situation even before the person has been exposed to it. This includes physical, spiritual, and psychological reactions.

5 The Bodhisattva intrinsically knows if a person is likely to accomplish their Zen spiritual goals in their current lifetime. Regardless of this knowledge, the Zen Bodhisattva proceeds with the assumption that every Cultivator can achieve enlightenment in one historic lifetime.

6 The Bodhisattva can instantly perceive the various particles and energy that go together to make up the phenomenal world. He is able to experience their interplay and essence. This allows him to intimately contact people, places, and things across time and space.

7 This is an awareness of the existence of different dimensions and the manner in which to contact them. Multidimensional awareness leads to the ability to travel from one to another and exist outside of the consensual at will.

8 This power allows the Bodhisattva to see the inner workings of the universe and determine what will bring harmony and clarity to it and what will not. Ancient Buddhists described this as a kind of subatomic sight that illuminated the "specks of dust that make up the world." The Three Worlds are the worlds of heaven, earth, and man. The Eight Places are the eight dimensions that go together to make up the Three Worlds.

9 This is an important skill for the Bodhisattva. With it, he is able to determine when the Karma of an event will exhaust itself. This can be negative as well as positive

Karma. A "man of excellent virtue" is an archaic Chinese reference that represents a man who patterns his life and behavior after the workings of the Cosmos. In Zen, inspired Bodhisattvas that go about their work with verve and dedication are called Men of Excellent Virtue.

10 The Bodhisattva is able to look at any spiritual technique or practice and determine its worth and outcome. He has complete knowledge of all types of meditation experiences, enlightenments, levels, and states of consciousness and mystic accomplishments. He also is able to make corrections on any spiritual practice. This power enables him to determine the worth of religious texts and expressions of devotional art. The Bodhisattva is able to judge the spiritual impact of music, color, speech, dance, and all kinds of physical expression.

CANTO XXVIII

THE PERFECTION OF DHARMA REALIZATION

The tenth Perfection is the practice of Dharma Realization.

What does it mean to practice the virtue of Dharma
    realization?

Hear this, brothers:
You must understand this teaching,
Because this teaching points to the mind,
No place else,
No thing,
No other.

The realization that I speak of now
Is the knowledge of
The content, definition, and goals
Of all methods,
All teachings,
All Dharmas.
In this stage of development,
The awakening being moves

From an earthly to a transcendental perspective
And peers into the heart of any given law
And discerns what is useful about it and what is not,
Discarding the cankerous secretions that do not
   point to the mind.

COMMENTARY

Zen Mind: The Bodhisattva who practices the virtue of Dharma Realization is the true guardian of the Buddha's message. He is a gatekeeper of the authentic Buddhist way who has complete knowledge of any and all methods of Zen Buddhist spiritual practice. In fact, his skill goes beyond the Zen Way to include all forms of Buddhism.

Zen Body: Over time, even the clearest of signals can pick up static. If the static is allowed to accumulate, eventually the signal is garbled beyond understanding. The accumulation of static is a natural outcome of life in the phenomenal world. Simply put, there is no way around it. It is a natural human reaction to be concerned with the correctness of spiritual practice. Sometimes this concern can lead to real fear that one is being led astray.

From a practical perspective, the Zen Cultivator assumes that some kind of interference is inevitable and should not be feared. If a Bodhisattva or Zen Master is not readily available to correct any deviation from the path, you must rely on the intuitive mind to help you make corrections. When in the presence of a true Zen teacher, heed his instructions. With authentic instruction, more is going on than you can consciously realize.

Zen Hand: To peer into the heart of a Dharma precept or practice entails becoming absorbed into it, and it into you. This requires the ability to enter into mystic union with any object of contemplation while maintaining a dual perspective. This is an advanced concept. To be in the mystic throes of an event while consciously choosing to remain partially aloof is a marvelous accomplishment.

Zen Heart: The Perfection of Dharma Realization elevates mystic, religious, and spiritual experience to the level of high art. Simply put, mystics experience, but often cannot communicate their experiences. Artists communicate, but frequently have nothing much to say or experience difficulty in accessing what is in their heart. With the practice of Dharma Realization, you become both, mystic and artist, able to effectively communicate the wonders of the mystic realm in a myriad of ways.

CANTO XXIX

As you sail onward and move toward the other shore,
You will encounter the lands of joy, purity, radiance,
    thoughts,
And others that I will address later.
For now,
Go forward and make yourself a fit place
For the Ten Perfections to manifest.
Craft of yourself a hollow vessel
With emptiness that can only be experienced
By looking directly at the mind,
By looking directly at the Buddha.

COMMENTARY

Zen Mind: The other shore, the one away from illusion and ignorance of the true nature of the universe, is a wondrous destination. Yet, the true Zen Cultivator knows that the "other shore" is in his own heart. Open it and the Buddha will be there.

Zen Body: Making yourself a fit receptacle for the Buddhist mysteries to unfold involves a coordination of all of the various aspects of your life. The Zen Way is to gently organize all behavior and activity into a unified spiritual practice.

Zen Hand: As a matter of technique, meditate on the emptiness of a circle or sphere. Buddhists have, for centuries, used the emptiness of space as a model for meditation on the essential emptiness of phenomenon. Using it as a means of opening yourself up to the experience of the Buddha Mind is, likewise, appropriate.

Zen Heart: You are a vessel traveling a noble course. Your thoughts, behavior, and intent motivate, guide, and sustain you on your journey. This is a journey into the self. With the soul as your companion and teacher, you will arrive at joy, purity, radiance, and Cosmic thought. What could be better?

SERMON THREE

SERMON ON MIND-TO-MIND TRANSMISSION

THE EIGHTEEN HANDS
MEDITATIVE TECHNIQUE

The "Sermon on Mind-to-Mind Transmission" is one of the most important in the Zen oral tradition. Among other esoteric concepts discussed, including the subjects of mind and spontaneity, is the Zen meditative technique of transformative movement called the Eighteen Hands. In order to more fully appreciate this seminal development, a working knowledge of its history, evolution, structure, and symbolism is appropriate. It is my hope that this survey will also help consolidate much of what has already been presented.

THE BENEFITS OF ZEN

The practice of any devotional path has a profound effect upon the life and bodymind of the adherent. Though many of these effects represent intangibles, the practical benefits of devotion help sustain the adherent during spiritual work and inform every aspect of his life. The benefits of practicing the original Zen of Ta-Mo include:

- Profound levels of relaxation, awareness, and ease,
- Increased mental and physical discipline,

- Increased mental and physical strength and control,
- The generation of a self-sustaining positive mental attitude,
- Elevated levels of optimism and compassion,
- Improved health and wellness,
- Dramatically enhanced intuition,
- Elevated levels of spontaneity and creativity,
- The ability to find great joy in everyday living,
- The discovery of life's deeper meanings,
- The evolution of a life affirming spirituality.

The tools employed by Zen Cultivators to achieve these benefits are known as the Three Jeweled Treasures of the Shaolin Temple and the Three Treasures of Zen. They are:

- Zen contemplation and meditation
- Spiritual *qigong* or life-force *yoga*
- Transformative Movement.

While each of the Three Jewels stands alone as a field of study, they form a method with overlapping centers in which each facet informs and supports the other. Ta-Mo created them to be a self-correcting dynamic wherein the regular practice of each prevented deviation from the true Zen Way. Traditionally, Zen Buddhists regard the totality of all three, as well as their subsets, as—simply— Zen. The "Sermon on Mind-to-Mind Transmission" details the importance of the original method of Zen transformative movement and spiritual *qigong* known as Ta-Mo's Eighteen Hands or the Eighteen Hands of the

Saint (Chinese: *shih-pa lohan shou ma-tzu or shih-pa lohan shou-ch'an*). Taken together, they form the heart and soul of Zen cultivation and mind-to-mind instruction.

THE HISTORY OF THE EIGHTEEN HANDS

Oral tradition maintains a large number of stories concerning the history and development of the Eighteen Hands. Most begin in the land of Ta-Mo's birth. Both the historic Buddha and Ta-Mo came from the *ksatreya,* or warrior class, of ancient India. As such, they were highly skilled in the arts of strategy, leadership, and combat. Even in war, the elite members of this class dedicated themselves to the general welfare of society and higher spiritual goals. Their symbol was the *vajra,* or thunderbolt, an imposing three-sided mace replete with small spikes and a sturdy handle. Wielding such a weapon took the kind of great strength and skill that was the lifeblood of the warriors' way. Soon the entire war art of the *ksatreya* was associated with the weapon and became known as the *vajra-mukti,* or Thunderbolt Fist Way.

When not campaigning, the warriors maintained and honed their skills by practicing lengthy and complex sequences of simulated attack and defense. These long sequences were called *nata* and were composed of shorter routines of shadow fighting known as *pratima.* Ancient Hinduism had already established the tradition of practicing *nata* and *pratima* as a means of exploring the depths of the mind and awakening profound spiritual wisdom. On the surface, warriors practiced these movement sequences to keep fit and preserve vital fighting skills. At an advanced level, however, they used their skills as a meditation on the totality of the self and an investigation into its inner workings. Essentially, this practice involved a solo reenactment of an actual combat situation. The warrior would infuse as much realism and meaning as possible into the reenactment. This included all of the emotion and energy of the situation. Fear, rage, heroism, panic, and triumph were part of the process. Even hatred of the enemy and joy at his destruction were important. The goal was to make it as real as possible. Once this one-man play commenced, the warrior would engage a meditative state and observe the inner workings of their mind. They would explore any thought or emotion that arose during and after the reenactment in an attempt to resolve self-centeredness, preconceptions, and life-negating illusions. In many ways, this spiritual combat was as dangerous as the real thing. The catharsis brought on by engineering a complete experience of primal fears creates an environment where only the strong survive.

What's important about this for the purposes of our discussion is that Ta-Mo, the son of a warrior prince, regularly engaged in this kind of spiritual practice as a part of his personal ethos. It would have a significant influence on the creation of Zen.

The ruling culture of pre-Zen China was also built on martial virtue, as well as the teachings of Confucius and Lao-Tzu. Yet, at the time of Ta-Mo's arrival from the west, the philosophy known as Taoism held prominence. It regarded man as the embodiment of the creative force in the universe. Taoism also emphasized man's stewardship of the world and the sacred importance of nature. Taoist Cultivators explored the natural world around them searching for the interplay of *yin* and *yang*, the receptive and creative forces of nature. They practiced a wide variety of meditation techniques and regularly engaged in *qigong* as a means of refining their bodies, minds, and spirits. Taoists sought to physically embody the Great Tao and cultivate an endless connection to the Source of Life. Literally every facet of Chinese life was influenced by the practice of *qigong* and meditation. Painting, poetry, politics, music, business, and education all employed contemplative and yogic practices. Even the millennia old Chinese martial tradition, just like their Indian counterparts, employed complex meditation and exercises designed to boost and refine the life force. It would be this world that Ta-Mo would encounter on his journey to the Shaolin Temple. The experience would fundamentally alter his philosophical perspective.

A MEETING OF TWO PHILOSOPHIES

In order to more fully understand what occurred when the Indian Buddhism of Ta-Mo met with a Chinese culture philosophically entrenched in Taoist ideals, it might be helpful to, by way of comparison, list some of the salient features of each.

Indian Buddhism At The Time Of Ta-Mo
- Philosophically pedantic and sectarian,
- Viewed Karma as a negative, blind, and unyielding machine
- Spiritual practice that emphasized a profound turning inward,
- Emphasized the evils of illusion,
- Emphasized the necessity of purging illusion from the being,
- Stressed the need to behold ultimate truth,
- Sought complete release from the consensual world,
- Focused on the importance of an established Buddhist community,
- Regarded that community as essential to achieving spiritual goals,
- Sought release from the cycle of birth and death,
- Looked to the mind for the secret of unity with the Ultimate.

Indigenous Taoism At The Time Of Ta-Mo
- Philosophically relaxed; laissez faire,
- Saw Karma as malleable and neither good nor bad,

- Spiritual practices emphasizing a profound turning outward,
- Embraced the mystery of illusion as something to be managed,
- Emphasized cultivation of the Tao as a way to lessen illusions' effects,
- Ultimate Truth appears of its own accord,
- Embraced the consensual world as a reflection of the Tao,
- Focused on the individual striving for spiritual excellence,
- Regarded community as unnecessary for cultivating spirituality,
- Revered the cycle of birth and death,
- Looked to nature to discover the secret of unity with the Ultimate.

According to oral tradition, Ta-Mo was greatly impacted by the people and customs of China. The Patriarch was exposed to many methods of meditation, *qigong*, and cultivation during his travels. As Buddhist teachers before him had done, Ta-Mo evaluated each of these indigenous methods according to the Dharma standard. Some he saw as useful, while others he declared unsuitable for supporting Buddhist practice. He studied the Chinese classics in general and the *Tao Te Ching* in particular. By the time he arrived at the Shaolin Temple, his philosophical approach was already in transition.

Ta-Mo expected to find a vibrant Buddhist community when he arrived at Song Mountain. Instead, he found a community in disarray. Ta-Mo set about instilling a rigid training regimen replete with long hours of seated meditation and mindful labor. He also began lecturing the monks on the complex tenets of the Indian Buddhism of the time. However, though the monks were willing, they could not grasp the overburdened and obtuse sectarian Buddhist philosophy that he presented. Buddhism had migrated to China in preceding years, to be sure, but in attempting to grasp what was essentially a foreign philosophy, Chinese Buddhist converts had misinterpreted and confused many parts of the Buddhist message. Ta-Mo's efforts to untie this Gordian knot remained frustrated until, during a mystical experience of profound illumination, he beheld the clarity of a more direct approach to awakening that transcended culture and confusion. This was to become the formal seated practice of Zen.

Ta-Mo presented his discovery to the Buddhist community at the Shaolin Temple, but the simplicity and directness of it only made matters worse. Still, the Chinese monks endeavored to follow the instructions of the Indian Patriarch and redoubled their spiritual efforts. Ta-Mo resolved to solve the problem. For several years, he observed the monks during practice, work, and rest. He participated in Chinese *qigong*, physical culture exercises, art, music, and literature in an attempt to understand the needs of his new Buddhist community.

Then, during a period of sustained illumination, he solved the problem. It was at this time that Ta-Mo formulated a more expansive concept of mind that revealed the need to create a moving Zen.

TA-MO'S EIGHTEEN HANDS

Using *qigong* exercises he had learned during his travels through China, Ta-Mo extensively reworked a *nata* he had practiced during his early days as a *ksatreya* warrior in his native land. The *nata* was called the *ashtada-savit-jaya,* or The Eighteen Victorious Subduings. What emerged from this reworking was not an Indian method, but a new paradigm that reflected the totality of the Zen synthesis. The activities were also possessed of a character that was distinctively Chinese. This was the creation of the Eighteen Hands of the Saint. This set of moving exercises contained the complete essence of Zen and radically transformed the body, mind, and consciousness of the Cultivator. This transformation, mystical in the extreme, protects the Cultivator, accelerates his spiritual endeavors, and insures success along the Zen path. Oral tradition holds that on the occasion of the very first introduction of the Eighteen Hands to the members of the Shaolin Temple, more than half of the monks in attendance achieved sudden awakening.

THE STRUCTURE AND SYMBOLISM OF THE EIGHTEEN HANDS MOVING ZEN

The Hands of the Saint are eighteen movement activities carefully designed to bring increasing levels of coherence to the bodymind of the Zen Cultivator. As this coherence is achieved, the movements themselves trigger intuitive insight into the nature of the consciousness and the self. Each of the eighteen exercises is a condensed experience of the many layers of Zen allowing the Cultivator to fully embody the entire philosophy. As a whole, the activities are:

- Eighteen physical movements,
- Eighteen individual and graduated Zen meditations,
- Representations of the eighteen progressive stages of a single thought,
- Eighteen breathing patterns,
- Eighteen *qigong* exercises for the cultivation of life-force energy,
- Eighteen symbolic spiritual hand gestures (*mudra*),
- Eighteen symbolic spiritual body postures (*ajmudra*).

In addition, Ta-Mo's eighteen exercises represent a collection of inner and outer spiritual skills possessed by a Bodhisattva warrior.

FURTHER DEVELOPMENT

The success of the Eighteen Hands as transformative physical movement was so overwhelming that Ta-Mo subsequently developed two other exercises. These short routines were also inspired by his earlier spiritual training in India. The *I chin ching* (Muscle Changing Classic) is designed to excite the *qi* energy of the bodymind to a high level, and the *shi sui ching* (Marrow Washing Classic) condenses the excited energy to the bone marrow of the Cultivator as a means of nourishing the blood. Both activities are used to promote bodymind health and wellness and focus meditative states. They are also used to induce emotional catharsis, train breath control, and cleanse the energy channels of the bodymind.

The Eighteen Hands of Ta-Mo continued to evolve long after his passing, but their use and purpose as movement that engineers a spiritual transformation remained the same. Over time, the original eighteen exercises grew to seventy-two; the seventy-two grew to 108; the 108 grew to 365 movements. Eventually, the transformative movement activities were grouped according to their name, spiritual usage, and quality of motion. It was from this body of moving Zen activities that the entire Shaolin art of *chuan-fa,* or Fist Way, evolved. Today, this is commonly called the Shaolin Temple Style of *kung-fu.*

For several generations, the Three Faceted Jewel of Zen remained intact and the philosophy flourished.

Tragically, sectarian infighting among Buddhists throughout China, as well as a period of cultural lassitude and political strife, led to the practice of Eighteen Hands moving Zen becoming separated from the practice of seated Zen. Successors in the Zen oral lineage refer to this as the period of Great Darkness and Confusion. The over-emphasis of seated contemplation led to the sequestering of moving Zen to the philosophical background. Some even came to despise the practice, seeing it as an unwanted diversion from Zen intellectual pursuits. Even the written record was altered to de-emphasize its significance. Continued infighting for doctrinal primacy among Buddhists in northern and southern China further muddied the waters. Soon, only Zen originalists practiced the Eighteen Hands. They became known as Followers of the Esoteric Zen Way and Priests of Hidden Zen. These practitioners of the original Zen approach retired from the mainstream Buddhist communities and, like their Taoist counterparts, sought to cultivate their path in solitude and secrecy. That having been said, the impact of the moving Zen of Ta-Mo had a tremendous impact on Chinese society, art, and culture that continues to be felt to the present day.

CANTO I

Hear me!
This is a secret transmission
That takes place outside of the scriptures.
It does not depend upon words or letters.
Instead,
It points directly at your soul
The soul of man.

Hear me!
See into your own nature
And attain Buddhahood.

Mind to mind.
No boundaries,
No enclosures,
No limits.
This is how we say it: Mind to Mind.

COMMENTARY

Zen Mind: This sermon lays out the specific method of mind-to-mind teaching that forms the core of the Zen Buddhist pedagogy. The foundation of this technique (see Canto IX in the "Sermon on the Ten Perfections") begins with a teaching method that can best be described as telepathic instruction. The student is expected to absorb the correct mode of being from the other members of his Buddhist community through a process of spiritual osmosis. Specific meditative and devotional techniques, however, are taught in verbal one-on-one sessions between the Zen student and his Master.

This method of transmitting the Dharma has its roots in ancient Chinese and Indian philosophy and is a direct result of wisdom gained by awakened beings of that distant past. Once awakened, these beings directly experienced the true unity of the inside and outside worlds of normal perception. To them, the notion of the subjective and objective was fundamentally changed. Thinking and behaving from this new ground of awareness gave rise to a unique view of consciousness. Likewise, the methods that grew out of this new mode of

186

consciousness have properties that are unique to it. In every sense, it is a special transmission.

Zen Body: The life of a Zen Cultivator revolves around the refinement of both mind and consciousness. All activity, no matter how mundane in appearance, is an opportunity to glimpse the Original Nature. To live a contemplative lifestyle supports the formal practice of refining the mind and consciousness.

Zen Hand: Masters in the Zen tradition will recite various cantos from Ta-Mo's sermons as a teaching technique. The idea of a "secret" oral transmission of knowledge begins, first, as a private teaching in which the Master adjusts and alters the meditative or devotional Zen technique to fit the gifts and deficits of the individual student. The implication for the student is one of profound intimacy with the Master, the method and the verse itself. Also implied is the notion that each student will take something away from the recitation of the sermon that is unique to them and their needs at the moment.

Zen Heart: The unlimited nature of "mind" without boundaries or limits refers both to the many ways in which consciousness is employed in Zen and the many levels of consciousness experienced and refined by the Cultivator. More specifically, it is a Zen core belief that the phenomenon of consciousness, as well as its expression through the bodymind, is unlimited.

Even though the awakened beings of the Indian Buddhist past formulated a new view of consciousness, an enlightened Ta-Mo felt it necessary to put their theories to the test. Driven in part by his missionary zeal and association with the Buddhist University *Nalanda* in northern India, Ta-Mo sought to penetrate the "act and process of knowing." His own practice gave rise to an even more expansive and sophisticated view of consciousness. His arrival in China continued to shape his approach as he was exposed to its art and culture, Taoist philosophy, and ancient Chinese methods of spiritual cultivation. The resulting theories of the mind, consciousness, subconscious, and dynamic thought became the foundations of Zen Buddhist psychology.

CANTO II

Heaven, Man, and Earth.
All that we encounter in these three places
Comes from the mind.

Those awakened beings
Of the past, present, and future
Realized this
And were able to grasp its significance.
Hence, they were able to teach
One mind to another mind
By employing physical movements filled with intent.
They used displays, shapes, focused sounds, and
    clear emotions.
They used conundrums, simple and profound
    gestures.
Thus, with their mind,
They move
Heaven, Man, and Earth.
That is how we say it.
Mind to Mind.

COMMENTARY

Zen Mind: The Zen concept of mind is an expansive one. Mind is distinct from consciousness and begins with the premise that the mind and body form a natural unity. Conventional discourse commonly refers to a mind-body split and the need to join the mind to the body in order to enhance the experience of life. To the Zen Buddhist, however, the notion of a split that must be rectified is nonsense. (Hence, my frequent use of the neologism "bodymind.")

To a Cultivator of the Zen Way, all is mind. This includes all physical movements, sensations, feelings, thoughts, impulses, mental and physical reactions, memories, intent, emotions, and will. The fingers do not move over the piano keys, for example; only the mind moves. The question is one of primacy. That is, which component part of mind is exerting the most influence over the human organism at any given point in space and time. Consciousness, on the other hand, is the backdrop against which these parts shift, move, and vie for top billing. The consciousness is also the motive energy of the mind. This energy can be sensed and experienced by utilizing one or more of the component parts of the bodymind as an object of meditation. Mind, in this context, is the complete experience of the bodymind components as a total gestalt. To explore consciousness is to explore the energetic glue that holds mind together.

Zen Body: The notion that all we do and encounter is merely a reflection of our mind and consciousness can radically alter the way we approach life. A Cultivator of the Zen Way examines each and every facet of his life from this perspective.

Zen Hand: Zen Masters precisely employ a wide range of physical movement and gesture to gain access to the bodymind of the student. Likewise, Zen students use physical movement to gain greater access to themselves. These kinds of Zen physical gestures and movements rely on a combination of a specific physical posture (*li*), a specific function of mind and will (*i*), and a specific configuration of life-force energy (*qi*). When each of these three factors is precisely balanced against the others, Zen Cultivators call it the Mother's Supreme Order. Under the influence of the Order, a Zen Master can employ coordinated actions of body movement, breath, imagination, energy, and intent to directly impact the mind and consciousness of the student. Since those actions are component parts of mind— and if the student is able to view the coordinated actions contemplatively— then the student will experience the Master teaching his mind directly.

Zen Heart: The Zen concept of mind is a refocusing of the concept of mind as expressed by the historic Buddha. Ta-Mo belonged to a lineage of Indian Buddhists that sought to return to this point of view. Unfortunately, this put Ta-Mo at odds with many of the contemporary Buddhists of his time. With regard to the mind and its workings, Zen emphasizes a keep-it-simple approach that reflects the Buddha's original spiritual message.

CANTO III

How is the Mind defined?
Mind!

How can I ask this question?
Mind!

How can you answer this question?
Mind!

Where does this question arise?
Mind!

Where does this question fall?
Mind!

All that you experience
Is the mind.

COMMENTARY

Zen Mind: During the oral recitation of this canto, the Zen Master forcefully puts the questions to his audience. The students in attendance sit silently with the question for several moments. When the Master feels that the time is right, he answers each of his own questions with a resounding, "Mind!" In practice, the questions are not answered. The tone of questioning, however, is of central importance and is an example of mind-to-mind teaching. The verbal interrogative tone generates and supports the Zen mental perspective. Specifically, this is a perspective of continuous curiosity, wonderment, and exploration that directs our human interest. This interest can be omnidirectional like a streetlamp, generally focused like a searchlight or finely focused like a laser. The questioning tone makes room for the intuition to speak to us.

Zen Body: Exploring the consciousness through the use of Zen curiosity is traditionally viewed as a Zen aid or crutch. Employing this curiosity during formal and informal practice will not reveal the Buddha Mind but will outline it, so to speak. It's as if you come to understand the motion and nature of an invisible powerboat by examining the wake it leaves on the lake's surface. Invariably, you begin to perceive things normally missed altogether. No matter how much wisdom and insight is produced by this approach, it is important to maintain a sense of your ultimate ignorance.

One way to bring the wisdom of insecurity to your everyday life is to eliminate as many verbal pronouncements of certitude as possible. For example, if you would normally say something like, "Classical music is better than rock and roll," change your response to reflect an attitude that is less definitive and omniscient. (After all, only someone who has heard *all* classical and rock music and possesses a method of determining a scientific state of "better-ness," could make such a pronouncement.) Your statement might then become, "I think classical music is better than rock and roll." This would make the statement self-referential, i.e. it tells us more about the person making the statement than it does about music.

A statement that fully embraces Zen doubt would be, "At my current level of ignorance and understanding, I seem to enjoy classical music better than rock and roll. But, I wonder… ." Statements of this kind leave the door open for new information, ideas, and feelings about music. Of course, merely talking this way won't accomplish much. But if you manage your daily affairs from this perspective, it will alter your life dramatically. Simply put, employing a sense of Zen doubt and curiosity in your everyday life leaves room for personal growth and expansion engendered by your intuition.

Zen Hand: The use of the questioning tone has many uses in Zen training. All of them, however, seek to expose the intimate details and intricate workings of the consciousness. This should not be confused with conventional intellectual investigation. The Zen student attempts to maintain a sense of questioning or doubt without succumbing to the need to have his doubt resolved. Zen Cultivators often refer to this as the "wisdom of insecurity." The goal is never to resolve the doubt or answer the question, but to bathe in the energy and spirit of the inquiry. It is this energy and spirit of inquiry that eventually leads to a complete experience of the Buddha Mind.

Historically, after Ta-Mo, the intuitive puzzles known as *kung-an*, or cases (*koan* in Japanese), became institutionalized techniques for controlling the quality, depth, and direction of the inquiry. This represented a divergence from the original Zen method that employs doubt in a light-handed manner as a means of naturally stabilizing practice.

Zen Heart: The Zen Way is one of intuitive investigation into the totality of the self. It relies on a state of openness and innocence where the wisdom of the deep inner self can move to the surface and make itself known. This state of openness and innocence is a prerequisite to authenticity.

CANTO IV

The Mind is the Buddha.
The Buddha is the Mind.

For countless ages,
This has been true.

For countless journeys
Taken step by step,
This has been true.

If it is not the Mind,
It is not the Buddha.

Search the world that is beyond the Mind
And you will not find the Buddha.

Search the young forest that is beyond the Mind
And you will not find awakening.

Search the mountain precipice that is beyond the Mind
And you will not find peace.

Search the cave that is beyond the mind
And you will not find bliss.

Questing here and questing there
Will not yield the Buddha
Will not yield bliss
Will not yield peace
Will not yield awakening.

Only Mind.
Only Mind.

COMMENTARY

Zen Mind: Zen seeks to engineer a complete experience of both the mind and the consciousness. This complete experience is a mystical blending of all aspects involved in experiencing any given object or event in spacetime. When this mystical blending, or *samadhi*, takes place, a new way of knowing emerges. This new way of knowing is employed in seeing the original self, beholding the Buddha Mind, and yielding the Buddha Nature.

This canto emphasizes the importance of the mind in the entire process of Zen cultivation. Traditionally, this begins with the cultivation of a mind that is fully open and profoundly aware. This is a mind greatly enhanced by specific Zen contemplative technique. The goal is to generate ever-increasing levels of mindfulness that can then be applied to the intuitive investigation of the self.

Mindfulness as an end product is less important than mindfulness as a tool. Authentic Zen mindfulness is a living skill that grows, as well as adapts to whatever situation presents itself during intuitive investigation.

The expansive Zen concept of mind points to a state of dynamic balance that begins with an enhanced perception that evolves in degrees. That is, one's mindful awareness of an object, a mental state, a sensation, emotion, or event can range from a partial to a total state of mindful awareness. The "step-by-step" experience of each degree of mindfulness is felt as equally profound and blissful being qualitative in nature. Said another way, every new increase in mindfulness feels as joyous and liberating as the last. Yet, at a later date, the depth of mindfulness can be evaluated by how flexible and adaptive it becomes. These graduated degrees of mindfulness, expressed in the canto as "the world—the young forest—the mountain precipice—the cave" also verbally leads the Zen contemplative to the place where his investigations must invariably take place, the expansive mind.

Zen Body: Living a life filled with mindful activity is considered informal Zen practice. Essentially, normal activity—the more mundane the better—is performed while practicing Tathagata Zen. The activity itself is performed deliberately and without a sense of haste. Completing the task is not the goal. Filling the bodymind with a dynamic balance of Tathagata Zen and the task itself is the goal. Each part of the task should be infused with as much mindfulness and equanimity as possible. As soon as distractions arise, the student labels it as "thinking" and gently brings the bodymind back to the activity.

Zen Hand: Mindfulness training in the Zen tradition usually takes place during the initial stages of Tathagata Zen practice. (See page 44.) According to oral tradition, Ta-Mo employed breathing as the meditative object when first teaching mindfulness.

Zen Heart: Mindfulness is a fundamental Zen attribute. Experiencing the gradual evolution of mindfulness is also central to the practice of Zen. It should be noted that it is possible for a dedicated student under the guidance of a skilled Master to encounter sudden awakening at any point along the journey of mindfulness. Once awakened, the student's depth of mindfulness becomes essential in managing and maintaining the awakened state. Simply put, a higher degree of mindfulness helps insure the clarity and longevity of the awakened state. Understanding the evolving process of mindfulness can better be understood by the following example.

The expansive nature of mind in Zen allows for a wide variety of objects and ideas that can be employed in meditation. When, as a Zen Meditator, you rest your focus upon an object of contemplation—a rose, for example—a lot of non-rose "stuff" floats in and out of your field of awareness and attention. This activity includes thoughts, feelings, ideas, and sensations that have absolutely nothing to do with the rose. Zen Buddhists refer to this activity as "mental contents." Mental contents, in this case, may involve the experience of your last meal, the discomfort of your clothing, thoughts of obligations, future plans, or even bad news received earlier in the day.

As you look at the rose, attempting to be as aware of it as possible, these and other mental contents present themselves for your attention. As you move from a state of less mindful awareness to ever-increasing levels of greater mindful awareness of the rose, you begin to be less and less aware of the non-rose mental contents. It's not that the non-rose stuff isn't making it into your conscious field, because it is; you are simply not as distracted by it. Your focus comes to rest more peacefully upon the rose, and the potential for distraction by the non-rose mental contents begins to decline. As you become more mindfully aware of the rose, it begins to take precedence in your awareness over non-rose mental contents. Your awareness of the rose begins to increase.

As your awareness of the rose increases, you will begin to feel as if the rose is filling up your bodymind. You will begin to feel as if the rose is, literally, inside of your bodymind. The rose fills you up, as it were, getting bigger and bigger. The colors of the rose get brighter, the textures take on life, and the sound of it, if the rose made a sound, would be rich and enveloping.

At this point, you begin to develop a quiet awe in the presence of the rose. It is such a simple thing that you have probably seen a hundred times before. But now, you are seeing it with a freshness that is totally new and pristine. It becomes thrilling, wondrous, and amazing. While this may not be a complete awareness of the rose, you are more keenly aware of it than you ever have been or ever thought possible.

When you first experience this level of mindfulness, it appears that everything else is blocked out. But as your mindful state increases, you discover that, indeed, you have not blocked everything else out. You become aware of all sorts of other mental contents, but those contents are not able to pull your focus away from resting on the rose. Your state comes to feel very private, as though the rose has your name and signature on it. It even begins to feel as though the rose is inside of you and you are inside the rose.

Even if the rose is crushed or perhaps not as beautiful as other roses, it is perfect. It looks exactly as it ought to.

As your mindfulness increases by degree, you begin to feel as though it's something that is unorganized or that it is something that you did not purposefully choose. Your Zen Master would tell you to allow the experience to unfold organically and warn you against attempting to control or organize it. Frequently, an increase in mindfulness feels almost like an accidental occurrence. Eventually, you will learn to manage this accident without interfering with it.

As the non-rose mental contents bother and distract you less and less, and you become more disengaged from those contents, the setting comes to include just you and the rose.

Bathed in a state of quiet awe, you will feel as if you could look at the rose forever. Sometimes, you are afraid even to breathe, as if the rose were so delicate that a rough breath might harm it. But, as your mindfulness increases, you come to understand that the experience of the rose will not be disturbed by your breath or any function of your bodymind. The rose takes on an eternal and indestructible quality. The paradox of the rose's existence quietly presents itself. The rose has always been this beautiful, while at the same time, you feel as if it has never been this beautiful before.

Finally, you come to understand that the rose is speaking to you in a language that only you can understand. This discourse builds quickly to a peak experience of mindfulness in which you become the rose. A merging, a meeting, and joining between you and your "rose experience" occurs. This peak experience can last several seconds or minutes. Eventually, you learn to sustain this peak of mindfulness for longer periods of time. When this occurs, you engineer a different state of mindfulness altogether that becomes the mystic state of *samadhi*.

It is important to understand that mindfulness is not an either/or experience. It is a Zen Way of Being that one can cultivate; it grows. It cannot be forced, but it can be invited. Unlike conventional concentration, it is not something that you willfully choose to do. It is not an exertion that you make or a demand made with a goal or reward in mind. The true cultivation of Zen mindfulness has a gentle understated quality. Your senses rest on the object of meditation without any thought of return, and you become so entranced by the object that the experience naturally evolves on its' own, becoming more and more complete.

The use of a rose in this description of the evolving degrees of mindfulness experienced by a Zen contemplative is an intentional device. I used it in an attempt to make the description of mindfulness and its evolution more accessible. While almost anything can be used as an object of meditation, great care must be taken. Different objects will yield different experiences. Depending upon the student and the situation, one object will be better suited for meditation than another. No single object, however simple, will be the best for everyone. A different way of saying that might be that the song a pianist chooses to play greatly affects the music that is produced. Sometimes a meditation object will facilitate a deep plunge into the bodymind of the Cultivator. At other times, it will only scratch the surface.

The Zen first taught by Ta-Mo at the Shaolin Temple on Song Mountain employs the bodymind in motion as the primary object of meditation. An individual, according to Zen Buddhist theory, is not a collection of parts. Rather, he is an integrated being whether he is fully aware of it or not. It is incorrect from this perspective to say that he comes to know the world through a collection of separate sense instruments and cognitive functions. Instead, the whole man is a single instrument of cognition. He is not simply a mind, but a body as well. The complete experience of physical movement, sensation, feeling, thought, impulse, mental and physical reaction, memory, intent, emotion, and will, as a single coherent expression grants the Zen Cultivator complete access to the landscape of their inner world and the totality of their Original Self. It is a hallmark of authentic Zen.

CANTO V

This is who we are.

To realize your own authentic and essential self
That exists spontaneously
Without effort or friction
Is to grasp the Mind.

Mind is bliss.
Mind is peace.
Mind is awakening.
Mind is Buddha.

This is who we are.

Mind.

That is how we teach
Mind to Mind
For there is no other way
To Buddha.

COMMENTARY

Zen Mind: The Buddha Mind is revealed in spontaneous activity. These are authentic activities filled with freshness, innocence, and wonder. Authenticity is a sophisticated state of play wherein life and your interaction with it are experienced as an enthusiastic free improvisation that draws upon your entire personality. Authentic moments that occur spontaneously emphasize the process and not the product. They are intrinsically satisfying and "freestanding." Though they are independent and exist without having a definitive purpose other than their existence, spontaneous activities generate bliss, peace of mind, confidence, and spiritual dignity.

Zen Body: The first and tenth lines of this canto are statements of Zen philosophical identity. The entire canto reminds us that in everything we do, everyone we meet and experience, we are mind. This is who we are.

Playful spontaneous activity is a hallmark of everyday Zen life. It is not uncommon for a Zen monk to momentarily become a child, hopping and skipping instead of walking or singing instead of speaking. Though conventional history portrays life at the ancient

Shaolin Temple as spartan and near joyless, the oral tradition recounts tales of laughter, good humor, and the occasional practical joke.

Zen Hand: Zen Buddhists since the time of Ta-Mo have recited this canto as a repetitive prayer, believing it to be power-laden. This kind of adjunct Zen meditation organizes the consciousness of the Meditator. The words are uttered at softer levels than normal conversational tone. Traditionally, the canto is repeated one hundred times in a sitting.

Zen Heart: At the heart of Zen is the belief that peace, bliss, tranquility, and enlightenment can be attained through its practice. Along the way, however, the Zen Cultivator experiences many other beneficial effects.

CANTO VI

Can I grasp the Mind?
No!

Can I grasp the Buddha?
No!

The space of no-space cannot be seized.
The form of no-form cannot be seized.

Control is an illusion.

No matter how hard one tries to see the Buddha
Beyond the Mind
It is impossible
Because the Buddha comes from your Mind
Because the Mind comes from the Buddha.

COMMENTARY

Zen Mind: The entire practice of Zen is something that cannot be forced. The Cultivator simply allows it to happen, so to speak. As such, the Zen Cultivator must behave as if all Zen devotional activities are the very key to his survival, while at the same time treating them with a sense of polite indifference. This makes for a unique spiritual perspective that balances spiritual urgency with a relaxed motivation. To wit: Zen is a profound seriousness that doesn't take itself too seriously.

Zen Body: A life guided by the Zen ideal is a life possessed of extreme patience that relinquishes the need to control situations. Rather, Cultivators of the Zen Way allow life to unfold as it wants and at its own speed. The poet William Blake expresses it best:

> He who binds to himself a joy
> Doth the winged life destroy;
> But he who kisses the joy as it flies
> Lives in Eternity's sun rise.

Zen Hand: The easiest way to experience a Zen sense of spontaneity and newness is to become involved in a hobby that you would normally not be interested in or an activity that you have absolutely no perceived talent for. It is vital from a Zen perspective to always be an involved and interested beginner in some activity so as to be an involved and interested beginner in life.

Zen Heart: The "space of no-space and form of no-form" refers to the concept of spontaneous and unpremeditated action amid a field of authenticity. Zen Cultivators often call it "non-doing" or "non-action" and use it, among other phrases, to describe a radical state of non-interference with the natural course of things wherein every action is spontaneous, free, and unintentional in the commonly accepted sense.

CANTO VII

THE EIGHTEEN HANDS OF THE LOHAN

Do not delude yourself.

Behold the Mind
And you
Behold the Buddha.

Awakened beings of the past, the present, and the
    future
Know the truth of this.
They instruct us to behold the Mind.

Delusion must be subdued
With the Eighteen Hands of the *Lohan*
So you won't scurry about
And miss your authentic Mind.

The authentic Mind is so very easy to miss
Even though the Buddha constantly presents it to you.

If you wear your mind like a coat
That belongs to someone else
You will be deceived.

If you become infatuated with the coat
That belongs to someone else
You will become lifeless.

If you imagine the Mind to be something
Other than the Buddha
You will miss the Mind.

If you imagine the Buddha to be something
Other than the Mind
You will miss the Buddha.

It is as simple as that.

COMMENTARY

Zen Mind: The teleologic ontology of Zen centers around the engineering of complete experience in a bodymind engaged in the act of perception. Said a simpler way, Zen employs the bodymind in motion as the object of meditation. The goal of that meditation is to mystically discover the Buddha Mind.

On this mystic journey you must claim true ownership of your mind and consciousness. You must not treat it as if it were a coat to be cleaned or clung to. If you become overly fascinated with the workings of the mind or the Zen methods used to examine it, then you will become spiritually lifeless and die.

Zen Body: Zen Buddhists faithfully balance the practice of moving Zen with seated Zen. Neither is considered to be superior to the other. A typical session of the Eighteen Hands can last anywhere from thirty minutes for beginners to three hours or more for advanced contemplatives. The entire set of eighteen activities is, traditionally, performed at least once a day.

Frequently, during a session of seated Zen, the Master in attendance will ask the student to perform one or more of the activities as a means of focusing the student's seated meditation and managing his contemplative experience.

Zen Hand: The Eighteen Hands are played mindfully without a sense of haste or worry. Each of them is regarded as a transcendental shape that exists invisibly within the Buddha Realm that is all around the Zen Cultivator. During execution of each exercise, the player gently rests his mind upon the shape and motion of his own body involved in the repetitive movement. Further, he imagines that he is gradually working his way into the transcendental shape that exists in the Buddha realm.

When he becomes distracted, he acknowledges the distraction as "thinking" and lovingly returns his attention to the exercise. Most often, the player's eyes are open and directed forward. As he moves from one Hand to the next in the series, the player maintains a contemplative attitude of introspection and passive observation of his own inner workings. He draws no conclusions about any image, thought, sensation, or distraction that may occur. The Zen Cultivator merely plays the Eighteen Hands against the reflective backdrop of his own consciousness.

Zen Heart: Cultivators of the Original Zen Way regard each of the eighteen Zen movements as being representative of Zen in its entirety. As such, the practice of the Eighteen Hands of the *Lohan* is regarded as a sacred activity. All of the knowledge and wisdom in the universe is locked away inside each and every cell of our bodyminds. The moving Zen of Ta-Mo provides us with the keys to unlocking that knowledge and wisdom, as well as the means of employing it to completely experience our Buddha Nature and of bringing all beings to awakening.

Canto VIII

Behold the Mind
By standing upright
Touching Heaven
And sinking into the Earth.

Subdue delusion
With fearlessness
And palms pushed forward.

Behold the Mind
While pushing the sky and the mountains.
Separate them and you will
See the authentic Mind
And find the Buddha.

Uproot the mountains
And you will find peace
That flows from a genuine place
Within the Mind.

Use this peace to find the Buddha.

Memorizing and reciting the words of a Buddha
Declaiming strings of wisdom
Is of no use whatsoever.

Visualizing the Buddha
Invoking his name
Calling him forth
Repeating his name to dissolve Karma
Is of no use whatsoever.

Following the rules and precepts of the Buddhist
     community
Measuring your behavior
Judging your moral character
All of this is useless.

Behold the Mind!
That is the only answer.

COMMENTARY

Zen Mind: The first of Ta-Mo's Eighteen Hands is called "Standing Upright and Sinking." It represents the Great Void from which all thought, action, and life is born. Mentally, the player identifies everything inside and outside of his perception with the Void. Man in the Zen tradition is seen as a product of the union of Heaven and Earth. The Void Stance, as it is sometimes called, symbolizes humanity stretched between the heavens and Earth, connecting and actualizing the power of each. This is regarded as a profound dynamic. This posture is also called the Buddha's Posture and is meant to symbolize the Buddha in a meditative state.

The second Hand is called "Pushing Palm" and symbolizes the emergence of a single human thought. It represents the initial strength of that thought as it first makes its way into the consciousness as an undifferentiated thing. Zen Buddhists regard this as the "Fearlessness of Thought" and also regard the bodymind posture itself as a representation of the fearlessness of the Buddha.

"Pushing Sky and Mountains" is the third exercise. It represents the expansive quality of the single thought as it grows to fill up your conscious mind. In that expansion, the mind can be glimpsed if one is relaxed, alert, and aware enough. At this stage, the thought has not yet taken root but begins to draw upon the resources of the central nervous system that is experiencing it. Zen monks often reflect upon the Chinese myth of *P'an K'u* who used his giant form to separate the sky from the surface of the planet in order for man to live upon the earth. On a deeper level, the postures formed by this exercise are meant to symbolize the Buddha summoning the heavens and the Earth to witness his awakening. It is considered to be a representation of the strength and stability of the awakened Buddha Mind that is unshakable in the face of illusion.

The fourth exercise is called "Uprooting Mountains" and represents the energy of the expansive thought as it condenses in the consciousness. This is the thought as it becomes more focused and coherent. This is also the movement and direction of the thought as it seeks to find a resting place within the consciousness. It symbolizes the Buddha immediately after his awakening as well as the seed of compassion that grew within his heart, calling upon him to teach the Dharma way to all of mankind.

Zen Body: Zen Cultivators attempt to live their lives as Zen meditation. As they go through their day, they observe the mind attempting to become aware of thoughts in one of the first four stages as enumerated by the first four of the eighteen exercises. The goal is to get as close to the root of a thought as is possible before it fully establishes itself and begins to involve the entire bodymind. In essence, Zen Cultivators measure all experience against the ruler of Ta-Mo's Eighteen Hands seeking to understand their own process of self-awareness.

Zen Hand: "Standing Upright and Sinking," is performed by standing relaxed and erect with the feet shoulder width apart and parallel. The Cultivator stands as still as is possible in an attempt to generate a profound sense of balance, poise, and equilibrium throughout his entire bodymind. Everything below the waist is thought to be so extremely heavy that, if left unchecked by the will, would plunge directly into the earth. From the waist upward is imagined to be light and buoyant. Were it not for the connection to the lower half of your bodymind, it would float quickly upward into the heavens. The player maintains a balance between the two feelings while allowing himself to become a fit receptacle and blank canvas for whatever is about to occur. After standing for a period of time, the player gently moves on to the second Hand.

"Pushing Palm" is performed by slowly lifting the opened hands to a position just in front of and level with the face. The palms are kept eight to twelve inches apart and the elbows roughly point toward the ground. The palms are then slowly pushed forward as if closing a door with both hands. By way of intent, the player pretends that he is pushing the heaviest object in the world without employing any physical strength whatsoever. Once the palms have completed their press forward, the wrists are relaxed, the hands leveled and drawn backwards toward the face. The pushing motion is repeated as a continuous movement. More often than not, the player exhales as the palms are pushed forward and inhales as they are drawn inward.

"Pushing Sky and Mountains" is performed by pressing one palm upward toward the ceiling while simultaneously pressing the other palm toward the floor. The position is then reversed by drawing both hands to a position in front of the chest and repeating the up and down press. When the hands come in toward the chest, the player gently inhales. As he separates his hands and pushes the palms to the floor and ceiling, he gently exhales.

"Uprooting Mountains" is performed by first lifting both hands upward to chest level and pointing the elbows to the sides. The forearms are parallel to the floor. One palm is turned to face forward while the other faces the breastbone, or "Heart Center." The hand facing forward presses in that direction while the other hand gently presses inward toward the breastbone. When the forward arm is almost straight and at the end of the press, both palms turn to face each other. The palms are then moved toward each other where they exchange places. The heart-pressing hand now pressing forward and the forward hand gently moves in toward the breastbone. The breathing is coordinated by inhaling as the hands move toward one another and by exhaling as they simultaneously press.

Zen Heart: This canto makes it plain that devotional acts, ultimately, count for nothing. Only by subduing illusion and beholding the mind can we expect to be awakened and find the Buddha. Moving Zen is designed to accomplish precisely that.

Canto IX

Look up!

Can you see the Dragon
Swirling and twisting his waist among the clouds?

That is Mind!
That is Buddha!

Your own Mind is the Dragon.
Your own Mind is the Buddha.
But the Dragon is not outside of you.

People think that the Dragon is without
But it is actually within.

There is no separation.

From the Dragon we learn to
Ride the winds and dance in the clouds
That leads us to the Mind
That leads us to the Buddha.

COMMENTARY

Zen Mind: In Zen both the mind and the Buddha are symbolized by the mythological Dragon, or *lung*. The Dragon is the beast that sleeps within the folds of the earth but rises to fly within the heavens. As such, he joins the energy of the two. The Dragon is also representative of the creative force of man who swirls and dances in the clouds displaying a tableau of the shapes and images of creation. The Dragon is so large and swift that it is almost impossible to see him in his entirety. However, if one employs an open and reflective state of mind, attempting to view the Dragon as a whole, then he will be able to discern the intricate movements and undulations of the beast. Indeed, he will be able to see the wind currents upon which the Dragon rides. The curving motion of the Dragon is called the "Wheel of Great Teaching." Whenever a Zen player performs the fifth of Ta-Mo's eighteen exercises, called "Dragon Twists His Waist," he is said to be "Turning the Great Wheel." It is symbolic of a complete experience of the workings of the mind and consciousness. In the evolution of a thought, this is a thought almost fully coherent and organized. Its details and intricacies are not, as yet, fully evident. However, the force of it as a created entity reverberates throughout the bodymind.

Zen Body: The Zen Cultivator attempts to live his day in a state of reflective awareness. That is, he holds his perception akin to a mirror that faithfully and completely reflects whatever is in its field. It is almost as if you were attempting to look at everything, even something directly in your line of sight, with your peripheral vision. The image of viewing the Dragon completely is a model for viewing life in its completeness.

Zen Hand: "Dragon Twist His Waist," the fifth of the eighteen exercises, is performed by holding the opened hands above the head in a special Zen configuration. The hands are held in the "Dragon's Gesture," which is formed by touching the tips of the thumbs together and touching the tips of the first fingers together creating a triangular viewing window with both hands. The thumbs form the base of the triangle and the forefingers form the sides. The joined hands are held over the head with the palms facing upward. The player looks upward through the window formed by his hands and gently twists his waist, turning his body alternately left and right. The player exhales as his waist twists to the sides and inhales as it untwists in between. In this position, the player attempts to view the heavens framed by his opened hands in a Zen reflective manner.

Zen Heart: A special Zen saying from the Shaolin Temple is, "From the Dragon we learn to ride the winds." The winds, in this case, are the components of mind moving, shifting, and changing against the backdrop of our own consciousness.

CANTO X

Dragons don't follow rules.
Dragons don't measure their behavior.
Dragons know that illusion and awareness
Is the same thing.

They keep no laws.
They break no laws.

They do not speak lies.
They do not speak the truth.

They do neither good nor evil.
They do not worship Buddhas.
They merely turn in on themselves
And balance the world.

First
They fly over the land
With their paws
Close to the ground.
Then they soar into the sky
Close to the heavens.

This is perfectly natural
Because the Dragon sleeps in the folds of the earth
Awakens
And soars into the sky.

This is his nature.

COMMENTARY

Zen Mind: After the Dragon flies among the clouds in the sky, he begins to look for a place of purchase where he can rest. This is the symbolism of the sixth exercise of moving Zen. The Dragon with its powerful talons flies low over the Earth looking for an appropriate place to land. With the overlapping hands resting on the lower abdomen, the player's bodymind forms the *tathata mudra* or Posture of Suchness. This refers to the complete embodiment of the true nature of all things. The thought, in our example, is not as yet fully apparent. In its incomplete state, it is still possible for the Cultivator to easily glimpse the formless and immutable Absolute before the thought can become part of the phenomenal realm.

Zen Body: The notion that illusion and awareness are merely two sides of the same coin can be disturbing to a fledgling Zen Cultivator. It implies that at some level, we must embrace our illusions if we are ever to be rid of them. At the point that we believe that we are about to eradicate illusion and achieve awareness, it will be revealed that, truly, the substance of one is the substance of the other. Attempt to be kind to your programming. It got you this far.

Zen Hand: The sixth of the Eighteen Hands is called "Dragon Kicks the Earth," or, simply, "Toe Kicking." From the feet paralleled and shoulder width stance of the previous exercises, the player draws one foot inward and places them together. He also overlaps his palms and places them on his lower abdomen. After collecting himself, the player gently and slowly kicks his foot forward to a height of about one to two feet above the ground. After the kick, he lets his foot swing backwards a bit and then repeats the kicking motion. After a designated number of repetitions, the player lowers his kicking foot to the floor and repeats the process with the other foot. Generally, when kicking forward the player inhales, and when allowing the foot to swing backwards, he exhales.

"Dragon Soaring Toward the Heavens," or "High Kicking," is the seventh moving Zen exercise. Begin by standing in a stable forward lunge posture known as the "Mountain Scaling Stance." Stand with your left foot slightly ahead of the right. Keep some width between your feet. Your feet should be flat with seventy percent of your weight on the front foot and thirty percent on the back one. Extend your right arm forward and palm upward as if gesturing toward the peaks of some distant mountain. From this position, kick your right leg upward with the toes pointed forward. After the kick, allow your leg to swing backwards and return to its original position. Generally, exhale when kicking the leg forward and inhale as it returns to the floor. Repeat as desired.

Zen Heart: To the Mind there is only perception. It doesn't mislead us intentionally. It is our unconscious allegiance to illusion that confuses and deludes us. To the Dragon, illusion and unconfused awareness is all the same thing. We have but to ride the winds like the Dragon does to understand the difference and completely behold the mind.

CANTO XI

Dragons paw the earth
Before taking flight.
Dragons sweep the ground with their tails.
Before taking flight.

Pawing and sweeping
Orders the natural world
So the Dragon can behave naturally.

You must see the truth of this.

The Mind is the Dragon.
The Dragon is the Mind.

Behold your essential nature,
Behold the Buddha,
Behold the Mind.

Paw the earth and sweep the ground.
Reveal the Mind and you will
Reveal the Buddha.

COMMENTARY

Zen Mind: The pawing and sweeping of the Dragon establishes order in a mind prone to discrimination. In the previous two exercises, "toe kicking" and "high kicking," the energy of the evolving thought reverberates between the earth and the heavens. In this case, these are metaphors for the energy of fully organized experience (Earth) and potential experience (heaven). "Dragon Hooks His Leg" and "Dragon Sweeps The Earth," the eighth and ninth exercises respectively, are symbolic of the final stages of the experienced thought before it begins to become part of the differentiated mind-stuff. This is the dividing line between the undifferentiated world of experience and the empirical world. At this juncture it is possible to see the "Supreme Wisdom" and the unifying nature of all existence. To see this wisdom is to glimpse the Buddha Mind.

Zen Body: Zen Buddhists often "look between" daily tasks and thoughts about the tasks as a way to glimpse the transition point between the unifying principle and the phenomena itself. This requires a profound skill at self-observance that each Zen Cultivator must train. One way to train this skill is to pretend that you are sitting in the rafters of the room you're in and intently watching yourself.

Zen Hand: "Dragon Hooks His Leg" is performed by using the foot to trace a small J-shaped hook on the ground to either side of the bodymind. The Cultivator stands poised to hook his leg and inhales. He then exhales and makes the small hooking motion. "Dragon Sweeps The Earth" is performed by alternately performing a vigorous backward sweeping motion with the entire leg. During this Hand, the Zen Cultivator endeavors to keep his breathing relaxed and natural.

Zen Heart: When a thought is experienced and begins to emerge in the field of consciousness, there is a time when it still belongs to the realm of the unifying Source of all existence. It has not yet taken root as a mental "thing." To view the consciousness in a mystic way—that is, to have a complete experience of the thought—is to see this transition point and be able to see the workings of the Buddha Mind in the phenomenal world. The reality of this experience is fundamental to Zen Buddhist thought.

CANTO XII

If a Dragon knows its nature,
Then why can't you see yours?

If you cannot naturally see your essential self
Then you must find a teacher
Who can directly point to the Mind
And touch it.

If you cannot find a teacher
Who can directly point to the Mind
And touch it in this way
Then your life will be wasted.

The cycle of birth and death
The cycle of living and dying
Can be stopped only
When the Mind stops
And beholds the Buddha;
Beholds itself.

That is how we say it.

COMMENTARY

Zen Mind: Your key to realizing your Buddha Nature is always present in the energy and workings of the mind. The mind knows its own nature. It observes, perceives, compares, and catalogues as it seeks to organize what it experiences; that is its nature. If you can directly experience the mind, i.e. see it clearly as it naturally functions, then you will realize your true self and essential nature.

Zen Body: As a daily exercise, the Zen Cultivator ponders the notion of the literal impossibility of death, even in the face of great tragedy and suffering. He observes the emotions and other workings of his bodymind as he does so. This serves many levels of Zen training.

Zen Hand: The Buddha Mind can be experienced in authentic, spontaneous, and natural actions. As a matter of course, it is important to be ready for the opportunity to "naturally" see the essential self against the backdrop of your inner workings. These are fleeting moments that appear as accidental flashes of intuition and awareness. The Zen Cultivator must learn to be prepared for these moments. In effect, he must learn to become aware of these accidental moments and be ready to manage them as they quickly unfold. Seated Zen builds this necessary skill.

Zen Heart: The idea that a true teacher is necessary to come to full accomplishment is ubiquitous in Zen. At the very least, a teacher must be skilled in the art of the Eighteen Hands and have come to a full mystic experience of their practice.

CANTO XIII

Ritual offerings order the bodymind.
Memorizing written wisdom shapes the bodymind.
Remembering historic Buddhas inspires the
    bodymind.
Basking in the symbolism of the Buddha brings
    comfort to the bodymind
And infuses it with abundant life-force energy.

When the Tiger is subdued
He reveals and flexes his claws
And straightens his waist.

Hold the Tiger firmly
And you
Behold the Mind.

Seize the moment like a Tiger
And you
Seize the Mind.

COMMENTARY

Zen Mind: The metaphor of both the Dragon and Tiger refer to different parts of the evolutionary process of a single thought, as well as the function of the thinking mind. When a thought is in the Dragon phase, it still possesses a quality that implies homelessness. That is, it appears to be a thing external to the bodymind perceiving it. This thought is generated by the interplay of consciousness and mind-stuff within the bodymind of the person experiencing it. When this thought begins to take up residence in the perceiver's mind and appears as part of the internal world, it has entered the Tiger phase of the thought. During the normal conscious perception of a non-Cultivator, this is the point when that human being becomes aware that they are thinking. However, the Zen Cultivator gradually builds skill at experiencing the earlier stages of thought. The tenth Hand of Ta-Mo is called "Young Tiger Flexes Claws," or "Golden Leopard Reveals Claws." This exercise is a metaphor for the specific stage of thought wherein the thought first takes root in the flow of consciousness.

Zen Body: The first stanza of this canto paints a picture of the devotional life of the Zen Buddhist within a temple setting. Mindfully engaging in ritual brings coherence and focus to the cultivator. Memorizing and reciting *sutra* passages serve as a guide to leading a Zen life. Great inspiration can be drawn from studying the life of the Buddha with contemplation upon the symbolism of his life bringing comfort in difficult times. Engaging in these activities results in an increase of spiritual vitality, energy, and focus. Zen Buddhists regard these collective activities as a means of turning their entire life into a spiritual *qigong*.

Zen Hand: "Young Tiger Flexes Claws" is performed by first standing in an attention posture with the arms crossed in front of the chest. The Cultivator then steps to one side in a wide stance called the "Tiger Subduing" or "Horse Riding" stance while simultaneously extending the arms to the sides as if opening a curtain. The hands, held in half-fists, form the shape of tiger paws. The Zen Cultivator then returns to the crossed-arms attention posture and repeats the movement on the other side. Generally, he inhales in the attention posture and exhales as he steps out and opens the imaginary curtain.

Zen Heart: Even if you are able to live a devoutly Buddhist life, the devotional life of a Zen Cultivator only helps to prepare you for the opportunity to behold the mind. Ultimately, that is the goal.

CANTO XIV

Pressing mountain tops
Exerts control over the Tiger.

Press the mountain peaks.
Seize the moment.
Seize the Mind.

The Tiger is the force of the bodymind
And the power of everyday consciousness.
When the Tiger runs free
You cannot behold the Mind.
Therefore, you cannot behold the Buddha.

The Shakyamuni's son was eaten by the Tiger.
He was able to recite ageless wisdom.
He followed all of the rules and regulations of the Sangha.
He kept the ancient rituals and preserved their meaning.
He was a spiritual warrior who could change his
     Sthana at will.
He basked in the glow of the Dharma.
But he was not liberated from the cycle of suffering.
He was a foolish child
Who could not see his own Mind.

COMMENTARY

Zen Mind: The Tiger in this context is the sum of mind components and the energy exerted by them as they compete for primacy within the field of consciousness. It is also the psychic momentum created by the interplay. The Tiger also represents mind-stuff that is available to everyday cognitive awareness. The eleventh Hand of Ta-Mo, "Pushing Mountain Tops," symbolizes the new thought as it prepares to further settle in the field of awareness. During the normal conscious awareness of a non-Cultivator, this is the point when they first become aware of the thought itself. Not yet fully formed, the indistinct thought can still be identified by its emotional quality. Usually, thoughts at this stage of development can easily be felt as either toxic or nourishing.

Zen Body: In the grips of illusion, the undisciplined mind can become confused about the essence of a thought. That is, toxicity or what is ultimately life negating, is mistaken for what is life-affirming or nourishing. On a day-to-day basis, the Zen Cultivator attempts to classify his habits, behavior, activities, thought, and speech as either toxic or nourishing. This yields great insight into the inner workings of the bodymind and shapes the relationship the Zen Buddhist has to the rest of his family and community.

Zen Hand: "Pressing Mountain Tops" is performed by first standing in an attention posture and then, alternately stepping into the Mountain Scaling Stance toward the left front and then to the right front. The Cultivator returns to his attention posture after each step. When stepping forward, the Zen Cultivator presses both palms toward the floor as if pushing upon the peaks of two mountains. The hands are turned so the fingers point toward each other. Generally, the Cultivator inhales in the attention posture and exhales as he steps forward and pushes downward. This gesture is sometimes called the *varada mudra*. It symbolizes the granting of a spiritual boon or wish. In this case, it is an embodied wish for the ability to control the force of thought and glimpse the Buddha Mind.

Zen Heart: As spiritual *qigong,* "Pressing Mountain Tops" tempers the energy of the newly arising thought. Ancient Chinese culture saw mountains as condensed and vibrant earth energy attempting to reach up and touch the heavens. The image of holding the mountains in check by pressing down on them is the symbolic basis of the eleventh Hand. The last stanza of the canto tells the story of the historic Buddha's son and the fate of those who cannot "restrain the mountains and subdue the Tiger." He was a model member of the Buddhist community in all regards, yet he was unable to maintain discipline enough to banish illusion from his bodymind and see his own Original Self. In Zen language, his life was devoured by his illusion driven thoughts.

CANTO XV

What is Mind?
Buddha is Mind!

What is the Buddha?
Mind is the Buddha!

What must I do to find the Buddha?
What must I do to find the Mind?

Discover and reclaim your essential nature
And you will find both.
Because your essential nature
Is Buddha Nature.
Can you see the truth of this?

COMMENTARY

Zen Mind: This stanza reaffirms the fundamental Zen
notion that the only way to awaken from the bonds of

illusion is to turn inward and glimpse your Original Self. Your essential nature is to be fully awake and aware enough to have a complete experience of all aspects of life. It is your birthright. You reclaim this birthright by freeing it from the imprisonment of illusion through the practice of Zen.

Zen Body: Glimpsing the truth of illusion can take place at any moment. Some of the best opportunities for self-discovery present themselves during normal daily activity. All that is required to mine these moments is a daily existence fully lived the Zen Way.

Zen Hand: As a matter of daily practice, the Zen Cultivator would routinely recite cantos of this kind aloud as a way to focus other devotional techniques. Within the oral tradition, some Masters will recite this Zen-affirming pronouncement between all other cantos in a given sermon. Usually a period of silent contemplation follows the final stanza so the Meditators in attendance can focus on the interrogative.

Zen Heart: The way to the Buddha is through a contemplative exploration of the mind and a complete experience of its inner workings.

CANTO XVI

How can you see
Your essential nature?

Observe the inner workings of the Mind
And you will be led to your essential nature.

How can you see
The inner workings of your Mind?

Straighten your waist
Like the subdued Tiger
And beat your wings
Like a wild goose
Flying out of the flock.

Let your Mind settle and rest
And you will begin to see how it
Turns things around,
Distorting them
Beyond description.

Distortions of life.
Distortions of death.

Everything that you normally experience
Is a dream.

Everything that you directly experience
Is Mind.

To directly experience your Mind
Is to discover your essential nature.

To directly experience your essential nature
Is to discover the Buddha.

COMMENTARY

Zen Mind: It is helpful in this examination to remember that the concept of mind in Zen is, in actual practice and approach, bodymind. Bodymind includes feelings, sensations, memories, and other mind-stuff. The second stanza of this canto can then be read as, "Observe the inner workings of the Bodymind /And you will be led to your essential nature." Profoundly, this is Zen.

The twelfth and thirteenth of the Eighteen Hands are, respectively, "Tiger Straightening its Waist" and "Wild Goose Beats Wings." Continuing to explore the life of a single thought in our example, the evolving thought takes root in the conscious field. It calls our attention to it by fully emerging from beneath the surface of normal awareness to appear in our field of mental perception. Said differently, the thought straightens up and we take notice of it. This is the Tiger's nature.

At this point in our mystic recognition of the thought, it begins to manifest a singularity that will, eventually, set it apart from the rest of our thoughts. The image of a single goose flying away from the rest of the flock communicates not only the uniqueness of the arisen thought but also its impending evolution within the community of thoughts inhabiting our consciousness. This is a perennial image in Zen influenced art, poetry, and drama.

Zen Body: The seventh stanza of this canto is a statement of basic Zen philosophy, as well as an indication of a specific esoteric meditation technique. Specifically, the Zen Cultivator engineers a belief system (i.e. convinces himself) that everything he sees and experiences in normal waking consciousness is, in reality, a dream. Behaving in this way helps introduce the Cultivator to the illusory nature of existence and the reality of his own participation in creating that illusion.

Zen Hand: The exercise known as "Tiger Straightens Waist" is played by stepping into a wide parallel stance while performing an inward gathering motion with both arms. The Cultivator maintains this wide stance for the next five exercises as a physical embodiment of a fully rooted thought. The Cultivator breathes in as the arms open wide and exhales as the arms gather inward. The gathering and embracing body posture forms the spiritual posture known as the "Tiger Subduing Buddha" *ajmudra.*

The next Hand, "Wild Goose Beats Wings," is played by gently throwing both hands upward as if they are flying into the heavens. As they are thrown upward, the player looks to the sky and imagines the lone goose breaking away from the flock to follow its own flight path. The player gently bends his arms back and forth while inhaling. The arms and gaze move upward and float downward during exhalations. The spiritually symbolic hand gestured heavenward is called the "Wild Goose" *mudra* and is known as the "Gesture of Differentiation."

Zen Heart: At the heart of all Zen practice is the idea of gaining intuitive insight into the inner workings of the totality of the mind. The fifth stanza of this canto fully encapsulates the Zen approach. To wit: Engineer a profound state of intuitive awareness by allowing the workings of the bodymind to unfold naturally without any interference. Then, with relaxed quiescence, mindfully observe the workings. This, human intelligence viewing itself at work, is the practical core of all Zen.

CANTO XVII

It is doubtful
That you can discover the Buddha by yourself.

To discover the Buddha by one's self
Takes a confluence of mysterious circumstances
That rarely occurs
And is rarely noticed.

A true teacher
Will know
When such a student presents himself
And
When such blessed circumstances occur.

Most people don't know
The Tao from the Tao.
They are mired in ignorance.

But, that rare person
Who authentically sees his essential nature
Does not need a teacher
Because he already knows.

THE WHOLE HEART OF ZEN

Night from day,
Dusk from sunrise,
And
This from that.

But, as I look out among you
My Dharma eyesight tells me
That you all must study and train.

You should bend the bow
And
Embrace the Tiger
To see the Mind work
Among the eight places
Of the world.

COMMENTARY

Zen Mind: Original Zen accepts the notion that a skilled teacher is necessary in guiding the student to full awakening. It also, however, acknowledges and reveres the idea that awakening can occur spontaneously without the presence of a flesh and blood teacher. This rare occurrence is something that every Zen Cultivator should be prepared for. In this way, even the movement of trees or the smell of grass can become the master that guides the student toward enlightenment.

The fourteenth Hand of Ta-Mo called "Bend the Bow and Embrace the Tiger" symbolically represents the stage of thought evolution in which the completed thought finishes differentiation and embraces its own uniqueness.

Zen Body: As a direct influence of Taoist philosophy, Zen Buddhists classify all phenomena into one of eight primordial types or elements. These elements each form a shape and energy that collectively establish the foundation of all existence. The elements are graphically represented by three-lined diagrams, or trigrams, and are referred to as a *kua*. Each *kua* consists of an arrangement of either broken or solid lines. The eight primordial elements are:

Heaven (*chien*): things expressive, strong, and outward flowing

Earth (*kun*): things receptive, weak, and inward flowing

Mountain (*ken*): things firmly planted and imbued with stillness

Marsh (*tui*): things joyous and pleasurable

☵ Water (*kan*): things menacing and gloomy

☲ Fire (*li*): things magnificent and awe inspiring

☳ Thunder (*chen*): things beginning to move and arouse attention

☴ Wind (*sun*): things displaying penetrating strength

   Much like their Taoist counterparts, followers of Zen intuitively observe the phenomenal world and watch for clues to the interplay of the eight primordial elements. In so doing, they attempt to divine the natural secrets of life as they play out against the panorama of existence. These eight elements also reveal layers of intent and influence within individual differentiated thoughts. These are the eight places that make up the world.

Zen Hand: "Bending the Bow" and "Embracing the Tiger" is the fourteenth Hand of Ta-Mo. Physically, the Cultivator draws an imaginary bow and arrow in eight different directions. The drawing motion is coordinated with an inhalation while the imaginary arrow is loosened during exhalation. As each arrow is released, the Cultivator imagines it penetrating one of the eight dimensions that overlap to form consensual reality. Each of these dimensions is named after one of the eight primordial elements. The *ajmudra*, or spiritually symbolic posture formed by this exercise, is often referred to as the Warrior Buddha.

Zen Heart: Most of this canto presents the concept of the importance of having a skilled teacher when exploring the Zen Way to enlightenment. Full awakening is frequently the result of a continuous series of partial enlightenments. Being so influenced by illusion, however, fledgling Cultivators can miss these moments of small awakening and lapse backwards into even deeper illusion. It is a Zen core belief that only a skilled teacher can prevent this from happening.

The ignorance, or *avidya*, mentioned in the fourth stanza of this canto, refers to deliberate and willful non-recognition of the Four Noble Truths of Buddhism. These truths concern *duhkha*. Some Buddhist traditions define *duhkha* as "suffering," but Zen Buddhists define it as "unrestrained friction." Specifically, the four truths are: 1) the truth of unrestrained friction, 2) the truth regarding the causes of unrestrained friction, 3) the truth of eliminating unrestrained friction, and 4) the truth of the methods that eliminate unrestrained friction. The specific methods that eliminate unrestrained friction, or suffering, are referred to as The Eightfold Path. Each of the directions employed in "Bend the Bow" and "Embrace the Tiger" symbolically represents one of these paths. Taken as a whole, they form the doctrinal bedrock of Zen practice.

The Zen Eightfold Path

The Eightfold Path is a collection of eight modes of being that form the heart of Buddhist activity. Each of these modes modifies normal human cognition and behavior. In so doing, behavior that begets unrestrained friction and causes human suffering is converted to behavior and cognition that puts the friction in check, thereby eliminating suffering. The words "right" and "perfect" are generally used in Western interpretations of the Eightfold path, i.e. right speech, perfect conduct, etc. This is unfortunate because it insinuates erroneous concepts into the precepts such as "right and wrong" or "perfect and imperfect." The eight modes of being are a dynamic interplay of human intent and action firmly rooted in the life-affirming philosophy of the historical Buddha.

Rather than relying upon single words such as "right" or "perfect," each of the eight paths can better be expressed in the following way:

"I will attempt to live my life by moving toward...

...a balanced wholeness of perspective that centers around the idea of achieving a complete experience of life.

...a balanced wholeness of resolve in which I deliberately move away from what is toxic and move toward that which is nourishing.

...a balanced wholeness of the manner, content, and intent of my speech.

...a balanced wholeness of life-affirming moral conduct.

...a balanced wholeness of a profession that affirms life and does not obstruct or negate it.

...a balanced wholeness of life-affirming spiritual activity.

...a balanced wholeness of mindful awareness and alertness as tools for profound living.

...a balanced wholeness of concentrated bodymind skills as tools for fully awakening to my Buddha Nature."

So much of current scholarship on Buddhism centers upon the devotionally austere and intellectually abstract. But Ta-Mo did not approve of or permit asceticism. Instead, he emphasized naturalness and moderation in all things. For instance, a Zen Cultivator may enjoy food tremendously as long as he eats to live and does not lapse into living in order to eat. Pleasurable activities of all kinds may be indulged in as long as the pursuit of pleasure does not govern behavior. One of the goals of the Eightfold Path, for example, is the ability to recognize the naturalness of pleasure and to completely experience the stimulation of the bodymind. That having been said, the Zen Cultivator also comes to recognize the deluded mind's judgment of naturalness and pleasure. As a consequence, he learns when to encourage pleasure and when to restrict it.

CANTO XVIII

Demons tell you that the accumulation of
Time and work
Is unnecessary
To behold the Buddha.
You must reach forward
And
Seize them
And subdue them.

Demons subvert the Buddhist teachings
By telling you that
Everyone has the Buddha Nature
So no one needs to acquire the skill of
Viewing the Mind.

They are liars!
They are devils!

They pervert the Buddha-Dharma.
They twist your perspective
Until you cannot use it.
They twist your perspective
Until you can no longer recognize it.

Illusion is their God.
Black becomes white.
White becomes black.

What a tragedy this is!

To sink deeply
Into the never-ending cycle
Of friction
Of birth
Of death

And

Never to realize your essential nature;
Never to realize your Mind;
Never to realize the Buddha.

COMMENTARY

Zen Mind: Zen Buddhists regard any coordinated
effort or consolidated entity that pulls you from the
Dharma path as a demon. In this case, a demon can be
corporeal in the consensual realm, a non-corporeal
force, imaginings, or even an unfortunate chain of

events. Demons can also be your own thoughts and doubts about the good sense of the Buddha's spiritual message. In modern parlance, being stressed out can be demonic as well as the predilection of succumbing to the influences of popular culture or public opinion.

Fundamentally, a Zen Buddhist must learn to stand on his own and forge a devotional discipline that is unique to him, yet still existing within the limits of Zen convention. Discovering how to best apply one's self to the practice of Zen within the intuitive limits of the Zen path yields a spiritual intensity that strengthens the character and personality of the Cultivator.

"Reaching Forward to Grab the Tiger" is the fifteenth Hand of Ta-Mo. It embodies that evolutionary stage of a thought that can best be described as mental energy being absorbed into physical tissue. It is a quickening in which the thought begins to affect the physiology of the thinker. It represents a consolidation of the various facets of the thought and a condensing or hardening of the thought as a definitive thing. Frequently, in the Zen tradition, this is called "Tiger Playing With a Ball."

Zen Body: Practically speaking, Zen Cultivators rely on new experiences as a way of reminding them of the freshness of direct experience. Simply put, doing something that you have never done before helps combat the demons and devils that would push you from the Zen Way of Life.

The fourth stanza of this canto points to the Zen process of routinely challenging ones deeply held beliefs as a means of escaping the totalitarian hardening of a life beset by illusion.

Zen Hand: "Reaching Forward to Grab the Tiger" is performed by inhaling and stretching both arms forward with the palms facing downward. While exhaling, the player gradually manifests a dynamic tension throughout his body as he slowly pulls his hands backwards to form tight fists that rest on the hips. The only part of the Cultivator's body that must remain placid and relaxed is his face and neck. At the conclusion of the exhalation, the Cultivator relaxes his body tension, reaches forward again, and repeats the exercise. The body and hand posture formed by this exercise is referred to as the *mudra* of "Unfailing Strength and Unshakable Confidence."

Zen Heart: This canto is quite clear about the consequences of allowing demons to distract you from the Dharma path. Possessing the dynamic strength of a spiritual warrior, as exemplified by the fifteenth Hand, is vital to the elimination of these spiritual impediments.

CANTO XIX

Are you an immortal being?
No!

Why aren't you an immortal being?
Because you haven't seen your Buddha Nature!

How can you be an immortal being?
By shedding mortality!

How can you shed your mortality?
By directly experiencing your essential nature;
Your Buddha Nature.

COMMENTARY

Zen Mind: When the Zen Cultivator can completely identify with the limitlessness of the self and function from that place, he is said to be shedding his mortality. The specific steps toward shedding mortality are supported by the Three Treasures of Zen and inform the Zen mindset.

The first step toward shedding mortality is the elimination of the obvious and unnecessary pain of mortal living and the expansion of the awareness of the limited self that is bound by illusion.

The second step is to penetrate the noise and confusion of the consensual reality-realm and glimpse the realm of the spirit. Once the spirit-realm is realized, the notion of the bodymind as a limited thing gives way to a sense of limitlessness. The intuitive becomes real. That is, far more real and authentic than reason and intellect.

The third step occurs when the Cultivator begins to experience the full force and power of the spirit-realm in a palpable way. This phase of mortality shedding requires renewed caution, discipline, and awareness on the part of the Zen Cultivator. There is the great danger of becoming overwhelmed by the power of the revealed spirit-realm. Elevated levels of focus, concentration, and mindfulness are required to navigate this phase.

The hallmarks of the fourth part of this process involve generating a profound reverence for and complete surrender to the unfolding process itself. This yields a new awareness of balance and harmony in which the Cultivator of the Zen Way slips past the discriminating mind altogether and begins to intimately connect with the essential self. As this occurs, the literal impossibility of death ceases to be an intellectual concept and emerges as a full part of the Cultivator's ground of being.

Zen Buddhists believe that this process is a perennial and cyclical dynamic that functions as a spiritual backdrop within all of us, whether we are aware of it or not. This dynamic constantly presents itself to us as an invitation to shed our mortality. In language borrowed directly from their Taoist counterparts, Zen Buddhists call this cyclical dynamic the Mothers' Supreme Order.

The Mothers' Supreme Order is a key concept in the Zen of Ta-Mo. Think of it as a song that repeatedly plays in the back of your mind. The process of shedding mortality is one in which the ambient noise of the illusory world is turned down so as to allow the once silent song to be heard. The act of listening to it gradually raises the volume level until it becomes loud enough to supplant the ambient noise. All that remains is to become harmonically and rhythmically entrained to the once silent song.

Zen Body: Zen Cultivators often speak of listening to the silent song as "experiencing the world slant." Practically applied, the Cultivator will, for example, look at objects with peripheral vision instead of direct line of sight. Listening to the silence between spoken words rather than listening to the words themselves or touching objects with the back of the hand instead of the fingertips are two other methods routinely employed by Cultivators. Exploring the truth of poetry and music are also common Zen approaches to hearing the silent song and, eventually, shedding mortality.

Zen Hand: The main formal Zen practice of shedding mortality taught by Ta-Mo at the Shaolin Temple bears the name of the cyclical dynamic that introduces Zen adherents to limitlessness—the Mothers' Supreme Order. This Zen spiritual training technique will be discussed in the commentary to Canto XXV.

Zen Heart: Shedding mortality and slipping past the cycle of birth and death is a Zen core belief that is often radically misunderstood. This is due, in large part, to the unfortunate separation of moving Zen from seated Zen practice.

By the time of the sixth Chinese patriarch *Hui-Neng*, it was common among Zen followers in southern China to routinely malign the practice of moving Zen. According to oral tradition, this group emphasized the distinctively dogmatic precept of spiritual exclusivity, among other anti-northern Zen ideas. Soon, southern Zen evolved a self-centered intelligentsia and orthodoxy characterized by just the kind of spiritual materialism that moving Zen was designed to prevent. In the language of Ta-Mo, these individuals were devils, demons, and disembodied spirits that deliberately prevented people from shedding their mortality.

CANTO XX

Mind!
Where is it?

Mind!
It is everywhere.

Mind!
It is always present.

Mind!
It is invisible to those who don't understand
    mortality.

Mind!
It is invisible to those who cannot see their essential
    nature.

Mind!
It is invisible to those who blindly recite sutras,
Follow rules for the sake of following rules
And
Mechanically do good deeds.

All of this is useless
Outside
Mind.

COMMENTARY

Zen Mind: This canto clearly emphasizes the Zen belief that everything is identified as mind. In brief, by the contemplative observance of our own mind, we gain intuitive insight into the Original Self that unerringly leads to the Buddha Mind.

Stanza four establishes new territory. The notion that everything is mind is radical enough. That mind is invisible to some and visible to others is an even more radical idea.

Zen Body: In actual practice, this canto is employed as a call and response activity in Zen communities. The Master loudly declaims the first line of stanzas one through six. After each declaration of "Mind!" the students in attendance recite the subsequent line or lines of the stanzas. The Master alone declaims the final stanza of this canto.

Zen Hand: As a specific Zen technique, the Cultivator strolls through familiar surroundings and allows his attention to rest on common objects such as trees, rocks, tables, chairs, and the like. When the Cultivator takes notice of an object, he points at the object and loudly mislabels it. For example, he might point to a rock and call it a bird. After dozens of objects have been mislabeled in this manner, the Cultivator continues pointing to random objects labeling each as "Mind!" Even fifteen minutes of such an activity can begin to alter the perception resulting in an awareness that two minds are at work in one body. One mind is experienced as the deluded mind while the other is identified in Zen tradition as the natural mind. The Cultivator endeavors to watch the minds at work in his field of perception.

Zen Heart: It is a Zen core belief that all devotional activity, no matter how well meaning and performed, is fundamentally empty and devoid of spiritual merit. Only through the mind can you come to know your Buddha Nature.

CANTO XXI

The Mind can be seen
In the thrashing of the Dragon's tail
As it seeks to smooth out the surface
Of your very being.

The Dragon is eternal and inexhaustible.
It can create the universe
When it flies among the clouds.

Words, smells, glimpses of light, tastes, and sounds;
Everything is created by the Dragon.

Your words are the Dragon's claws
Striking outward
First, one way
And then, another.

But, the authentic Mind is naturally awakened.
It cannot die or be blunted by ordinary life.

The natural Mind is balanced.
The natural Mind is poised.
The natural Mind is equal to itself.

The natural Mind is sacred.
The natural Mind is awake.
The natural Mind is aware.

COMMENTARY

Zen Mind: The image of the *lung* or Dragon emerges as that stage in a thought's evolution wherein the natural mind attempts, one last time, to throw off this new illusion. It also represents the fully rooted and differentiated thought rapidly expanding throughout the consciousness and becoming an integral part of the entire matrix of consciousness and mind-stuff. This is experienced as waves of oscillating nuance that grow omnidirectionally to fill all parts of the mind field. The thought is about to become part of the illusory world. The sixteenth Hand of Ta-Mo embodies this stage. It is called "The Dragon Thrashes its Tail."

The seventeenth Hand of Ta-Mo is called "The Dragon Strikes Out." Here the thought digs in and becomes a complete partner in the formation of illusion. The image is one of a Dragon striking out with its claws in all directions as it claims space and searches for primacy. In doing so, it becomes part of everything you think, say, or do. It becomes connected to memories from the past and sensations from the present. This is a thought that becomes woven into the very fabric of ordinary living. Yet, hidden beneath this fabric is the natural mind, which is the only way to the Buddha.

Zen Body: During normal activity, the Zen Cultivator regards every part of his life as sacred and attempts to infuse it with increasing levels of balance, poise, and equilibrium. He regards this as a kind of informal practice in which he lives his life as art. Only then can the natural mind surface and be seen.

Zen Hand: "Dragon Thrashes its Tail" is performed by first joining the hands to form the "Dragons' Gesture." (See the fifth Hand.) The player holds the joined hands in front of his body and begins to trace an infinity symbol in the air. The motion can be played in either a relaxed or vigorous manner. The player imagines that the continuous oscillating movement of the hands sends waves of connectivity in all directions. This, not unlike "Dragon Twist Waist," symbolically represents the turning of "The Wheel of Great Teaching." The player endeavors to allow his breath to unfold naturally as he performs this exercise.

Following this period of vigorous movement, the player decelerates and seamlessly moves on to the seventeenth Hand, called "Dragon Striking Out with Claws." Essentially, the player shifts from side to side gesturing with closed fists in a circular fashion. When twisting to the right, he traces a clockwise circle with his right fist. He traces a counterclockwise circle when twisting to the left. When a hand is circling upward, the player inhales, and when the fist circles downward, he exhales. The *ajmudra* formed by this exercise is called the posture "Defiance and Protection."

Zen Heart: Uncovering the natural mind is the goal of Zen practice in general and moving Zen in particular.

CANTO XXII

The Mind that turns in on itself
Is the Tathagata.

It demonstrates its limitlessness
By turning in on itself
In a continuous cycle
Of endless creation
And condensed movement
That gives rise to
Continuous enlightenment.

Everyone has the Buddha Mind.
Everyone has the Buddha Nature.

Let the Dragon teach you how to ride the winds
And the awareness of the Buddha Mind
Becomes endless.

See your nature in the winds
And be enlightened.

There is no other way to the Tao path.

COMMENTARY

Zen Mind: The final stage of the evolving thought graphically displayed during the physical execution of the Eighteen Hands occurs when the thought becomes so well defined and entrenched in the consciousness that its opposite spontaneously appears. At this precise point of turning in on itself, the essence of the universe is revealed in a near-blinding instant. It is the last opportunity for the Zen Cultivator to glimpse his essential nature in the thought and behold the Buddha Mind.

Please remember, the Eighteen Hands are an exposition of the evolution of a single human thought. Each stage presents the Cultivator with an opportunity for full awakening. As we continually experience thought, we are continuously experiencing opportunities for enlightenment.

The eighteenth Hand is called the "Tathagata Turns Around and Views the Universe," or "Pivot the Mind and Push Forward." Both the body and hand posture formed by this exercise are called the "Thus-Gone and Thus-Perfected Buddha." It symbolically represents the full flowering of the Buddha Nature that resides within everyone.

Zen Body: Learning how to ride the winds begins with observing the consciousness and mind-stuff at work during seated Zen. Transformative moving Zen allows an even greater opportunity to directly experience the Dragon of mind-stuff and consciousness. The physically expressive art of *kung-fu* with its energetic punches and kicks is the vehicle employed by followers of the original Zen of Ta-Mo. They use *kung-fu* to observe the inner workings of the self and the roots of their own natures. Without learning how to ride the winds, there can be no authentic Zen.

Zen Hand: "Tathagata Turns and Views the Universe" is performed by gathering the arms and hands at the waist, stepping forward, and pushing the hands upward to mimic the motion of a lotus flower pushing upward through the mud to bloom. After completing one push, the player quickly turns around, gathers himself, and repeats the lotus pushing movement in the opposite direction. Breathing is kept relaxed and natural. As the player turns around between each physically symbolic blooming of the lotus, he attempts to catch a glimpse of the cosmic principle that lies at the heart of all Buddhist practice.

Zen Heart: Both the chance and the opportunity for a complete and sudden enlightenment is continuously being presented to everyone and anyone. Zen is radically inclusive, open, and nonjudgmental. Anyone who sincerely wishes to follow the Zen path of Ta-Mo can experience the Buddha in this one lifetime.

CANTO XXIII

Do not worship Buddhas.
Do not worship awakened beings.
Do not worship Bodhisattvas.

They are external spirits and wraiths

Because they are not you
Because they are not your essential self
Because they are not Mind.

Buddha is none of these
Buddha is formless
Buddha is the natural Mind.

Our Mind is nature
Our Nature is Mind
Our Mind is Buddha.

COMMENTARY

Zen Mind: Central to the spiritual life of a Zen Cultivator is the concept of self-reliance. Even in the oftentimes-complex search for awakening, the Cultivator must go it alone. While Ta-Mo emphasizes the need for a true teacher and the clearest methods for achieving awakening, the most important person is the Cultivator himself or herself. This level of spiritual independence is rarely seen in modern society, which constantly competes with your devotional goals. Still, if one is to succeed in Zen, the determination and discipline of a warrior is necessary.

Zen Body: Any activity that exerts independence or generates feelings of individualism supports formal Zen cultivation. That having been said, these activities should not take time away from Zen meditation.

Zen Hand: Many individuals approach the practice of Zen in a casual manner. This is not inappropriate because even a haphazard Zen practice can yield many benefits, such as improved health and memory. Plainly said, however, a haphazard or less than committed practice will simply not sustain the Zen spiritual quest.

Zen Heart: This entire canto re-emphasizes the Zen precept that looking for the Buddha outside of the mind is nothing more than a fruitless search.

CANTO XXIV

Devils, demons, and disembodied spirits abound.

They preach the emptiness of everything.
They preach the non-existence of Karma.

They hold morals and virtues as relative ideals
And justify their actions
By denying the existence of good and evil.

If you practice emptying your Mind
Before seeing your essential nature,
You will be consumed by yourself
And lost in hellish darkness.

If you practice emptying your Mind
Before seeing your essential nature,
You will have no root
And you will be adrift
Forever.

COMMENTARY

Zen Mind: In this canto, Ta-Mo warns his followers to beware of embracing a superficial understanding of illusion, awakening, meditation, and mortality. He is also warning them of those who propagate that kind of superficiality. Central to the philosophy of those described as devils and demons is the idea that the truth of illusion is not fixed but plastic. That is, illusion as a concept is malleable. One person's illusion is not another person's illusion. Furthermore, this difference is spiritually significant. Authentic Zen, however, which emphasizes putting an end to illusion, holds that the root of illusion is universal and does not vary from person to person. Said another way, demons emphasize differences while true Zen cultivators concern themselves with similarities.

The notion that illusion is variable and specific to an individual invariably leads to the premise that human nature, though flawed, is not fixed and, therefore, is capable of controllable and fundamental change in the absence of awakening, i.e. people are perfectible without full spiritual awareness. We have but to identify their specific illusion and address it with hard target techniques of behavior modification and formulaic emotional re-programming. Once this is accomplished, the individual penetrates the illusion that troubles them and they take a step away from imperfection. This runs contrary to the original Zen premise that people are already perfect to begin with. We have only to penetrate the root of illusion in its totality and glimpse our essential nature to realize the fact of this perfection.

The Zen of Ta-Mo realizes that man is predominantly driven by the forceful weight of illusion characterized by irrational impulses and, often anti-rational feelings and sentiments. Conquering these feelings and impulses takes great spiritual discipline, courage, and skill. It is frequently very difficult. Demons, on the other hand, advise you to believe that fundamental change is easy and perfectly natural if, to use a modern phrase, you "can get your head right." This superficial understanding that is characteristic of the disembodied spirit leads to sectarianism, self-loathing, pessimism, and all manner of ideological thinking that stifles the intuitive reasoning vitally important to beholding the Buddha Mind. This superficiality must be avoided at all costs.

Zen Body: The idea of avoiding demons while walking the Zen path involves maintaining a relaxed countenance along the way. Giving them too much attention only encourages them and attracts more of their disharmony. The Zen Cultivator combats these denizens by taking comfort and refuge in the good sense of the Buddhist message.

Zen Hand: Popular discourse on Zen meditation frequently includes the idea that Zen involves an emptying of the mind, thereby ridding it of illusion. However, this is not the original Zen Way.

In many ways, a mind that is deluded by illusion acts in a stiff and robotic fashion. As a result, all of our outward behavior becomes robotic. While this might sound bad at first blush, this robotic behavior is not entirely undesirable. For example, our robot got us out of bed this morning. It helped cleanse and feed our bodies. We could not drive our cars or obey the laws of our communities without the robot or the rationalizations that sustain it.

Zen philosophy holds that a Cultivator should, in a manner of speaking, treat his or her robot with kindness. After all, the robot managed to deliver the Cultivator to the tender mercies of the Zen Way.

To completely expunge the robotic tendencies of our being and the associated detritus from our minds would sever us from the life we have thus far created. It is within the folds of that created life that the clues to our awakening exist.

Zen Heart: Many people come to Zen in an attempt to counter the effects of an overwhelmingly negative self-image. Sadly, a negative self-image is the single biggest threat to survival in the consensual world. Zen philosophy considers this situation as a spiritual disease in which the afflicted has no root with which to draw nourishment. Such individuals come to regard their thoughts as impure and unworthy of even existing. It is a Zen core belief that each of us is part of the divinity that is the Buddha Mind. We have only to accept ourselves as we are with all of our gifts and deficits and surrender to the natural evolution of our lives. In this way, attempting to see our essential nature, we are able to reclaim our terrestrial safety and draw heavenly nourishment from the Zen Way of Life.

CANTO XXV

Purify your bodymind
By exciting your life force.
Direct it to move
Through the muscles of your arms and legs.
Condense it to your bones
And engage moving Zen.

This movement becomes the source of no-mind.
This movement becomes a forge and refuge.
This movement becomes the Mother's Supreme Order.
This movement transforms and points to the Mind.

Mind lives in the Buddha.
Buddha lives in the Mind.
Mind only is the Buddha.
Buddha only is the Mind.

Mind is not separate
From the flesh, bones, breath, and blood
Of the body.

Buddha cannot be realized if you seek it with Mind.
Do not seek it with the Mind

Because your idea of Mind is a thing
That is outside of your natural Mind.

Balance the Mind and the natural Mind will appear.

Bodymind movement that transforms you
Subdues the Mind-thing.
It calls the natural Mind forward.

Dharma Body
Buddha Mind.

This is the only path to awakening.

COMMENTARY

Zen Mind: This canto outlines the method by which the mind-thing or unnatural mind can be subdued and the natural mind called forward. This method is called the Mothers' Supreme Order, or Zen Ordering. This is also described in the Zen oral tradition as the method of shedding mortality. It accesses a cyclical dynamic of periods of delusion and wakefulness that is an integral part of humankind.

At its simplest, the Mothers' Supreme Order represents a projected balance of mental intent, physical expressiveness, and life-force energy within a specific routine of carefully designed transformative bodymind movement. It attempts to generate a frequency within the bodymind that is parallel to the frequency of the natural mind. If properly engineered, the power of the natural mind makes itself known to the Cultivator during the performance of the movement routine. It temporarily supplants the ordinary mind during this process. This event generates examples of complete experience, awakening, and all phases of the Zen experience. It serves as an accessible display of Zen standards, as examples of benchmarks in advanced cultivation, and as a kind of spiritual quality control that helps prevent the Cultivator from straying from the Zen path. It is regarded as a complete Zen method that connects to all other Zen methods.

Zen Body: The Mothers' Supreme Order is, generally speaking, applied to all of the moving Zen that evolved from the original Eighteen Hands of Ta-Mo. However, with a little practice, almost any physical activity can be approached in this way. While the transformative movement routines of moving Zen were designed with specific spiritual and energetic goals in mind, normal everyday activity can be elevated to mystic art when infused with the Order.

Zen Hand: The Zen practice of the Mothers' Supreme Order begins with the choosing of a specific transformative movement routine. This routine, well rehearsed and ritually imbued with symbolic meaning, is one that requires focus, skill, strength, and concentration to properly execute.

THE MOTHERS' SUPREME ORDER

• With the routine chosen, the player stands in preparation and attempts to engage a balanced mind. This is a mental state that is reflective, yet not completely passive. The player stands in a physical ready-posture that demonstrates poise and balance. It is taken as a means of engendering those qualities within the player. Any feelings of anticipation or worry are put to route. Within the closed system of the player and the Tao, a mind balanced in this way begins to generate mind-stuff against the field of consciousness.

• When a sense of balance, poise, and equilibrium is established, the player stabilizes his life-force energy at a spot three and one half inches below the navel and inward known as the *tan tien*, or lower heaven. The life-force energy of the bodymind is allowed to naturally collect and is not forced in any way. When the player feels as though he is getting physically heavier or is sinking into the ground, he moves on to the next part of the order.

• The player engages his intention by stimulating his imagination in accordance with the dictates and construction of the routine. If he is about to mimic the movement of water, for example, he begins to think of himself as fast-moving water. In essence, the player floods his conscious mind with imaginings that support his impending movement routine. For his intention to be fully realized, he must will himself to move as if he had no actual control over the process. This is akin to the Zen archer who physically draws the bow and sees the arrow striking the target over and over again in his imagination. This is the will to move.

• Intention becomes fully "alive" when the imaginings cause the player to spontaneously move. This is a call to direct action in which the player finds himself physically involved in the routine before he is aware of it. This kind of movement has a physically expressive and dramatic quality that separates it from ordinary activity.

• As a result of this intent-full physical movement, the player's life-force energy, or *qi*, is excited to a high level throughout his bodymind. As soon as the player becomes aware of this excitation, he endeavors to support it with pre-designated patterns of *qi* energy specifically designed to support and invigorate the movements contained in the routine. All of this results in a massive increase in the player's life-force energy in which he becomes a conduit for what Zen Cultivators call the *qi* of the Universal Principle.

• As greater amounts of life-force energy are channeled through the player, a commensurate amount of energy starts to gather in his tissues and bones. If the player is able to continue the movement routine while simultaneously surrendering to the *qi* collecting within him, he experiences a mystic state in which he glimpses the interconnectedness of all corners of life and creation. This experience is heralded by the sensation of small electrical shocks that stimulate and invigorate the bodymind.

• If the player can continue the routine in the face of these sensations, he experiences a deeper state of balance, poise, and equilibrium that starts the process anew. This signals the subduing of the deluded mind that is called *wu-hsin*, or innocence. *Wu-hsin*, sometimes translated as "no mind," signals the emergence of a complete naturalness and authenticity that is free from dualistic thinking. When this occurs, the player begins to believe that they are creating their pre-arranged physical movement routine for the very first time. Each movement is experienced as entirely fresh and new.

At this point in the process, the player feels strong, comforted, and protected as the natural mind expresses itself in an attempt to be heard. The player feels as though he is functioning from a place of unlimited awareness. With that comes the revelation of the deep inner movements of the Dragon and the Tiger, the very warp and woof of existence.

Zen Heart: Directly engaging the Mothers' Supreme Order during the practice of moving Zen introduces the Cultivator to the holographic nature of the entire universe. It also imbues the Cultivator with a palpable sense of the limitlessness of the universe, as well as his place in it.

CANTO XXVI

The word "Buddha" means
One who is awakened
One who is alert and
One who is purposefully aware.

Profoundly awake, alert, and aware
You move about and explore
Your reality realm.

The movement of your bodymind within
The reality realm is the object of your Zen.

Being profoundly awake, alert, and aware within
The movement of your bodymind
Is also Zen.

Seeing your essential nature as you physically move
    about
Exploring the reality realm
Is also Zen.

The Tao Path and the Tao Way are Zen.
The Mind is Zen and the Buddha is Zen.

This is mysterious
But, true.

Zen is the path, the object, the method, and the goal.

If you can see your essential nature
Everything is Zen.

COMMENTARY

Zen Mind: In this canto, Ta-Mo summarizes the entire subject of Zen philosophy and practice. He particularly emphasizes the importance of moving Zen in the quest for awakening.

Zen Body: This canto provides a wealth of inspiration on living a Zen life. With this focus, the verse may be rendered in this way:

> Live an awakened life in which you are
> alert and aware.
>
> Live your life with purpose and explore
> your world.

Experience as much of the world as is possible.

Your bodymind moving through life is your object of contemplation.

Your movement through life is Zen.

The exploration of yourself and your life is Zen.

Try to see your essential nature while living your life.

The path is the way and the way is the path.

Your mind is Zen and the Buddha is Zen.

Your life, as Zen, is the object, path, and method of awakening.

Mindfully live so you can see your essential nature.

See your essential nature and every aspect of living will become Zen.

Zen Hand: Stanzas two through five clearly define the use of transformative movement in Zen. The bodymind in motion is the object of the Zen meditation founded at the Shaolin Temple at Song Mountain. The reality realm is the consensual reality available to normal waking consciousness. The physical culture arts that evolved from Ta-Mo's original Eighteen Hands form a sophisticated system of bodymind wisdom. As a bodymind philosopher, the Zen Cultivator fuses the totality of the self with the wonders of the natural world. Thus forged, he plunges headlong into the nature of illusion, suffering, cognition, and awareness. He must move his bodymind; he must explore his environment; he must search for his original face and essential self. He must—body and soul—"be" Zen.

Zen Heart: The promise of Zen is universal and available to everyone regardless of age, gender, ethnicity, education, or religion. The philosophy of Ta-Mo is one of radical inclusion. It is nonjudgmental and completely adaptable to any life that embraces it. All that one must do is, well… do it. The Buddha's message is a simple one: Wake up! The message of Ta-Mo is likewise a simple one: Look to yourself. That is where you will find the Buddha. Those combined messages form the heart of the Zen life.

Reverend John A. Bright-Fey is initiated and ordained in several of the world's great religious traditions. He is the sole inheritor of more than two dozen privately held oral wisdom traditions. An accomplished Master of the Chinese martial arts, he is also the creator of the New Forest Way®, a groundbreaking paradigm that allows modern audiences greater access to the ancient wisdom traditions of China and Tibet, and the author of other books in the Whole Heart™ series and several books in the Morning Cup™ series.

ABOUT THE CALLIGRAPHY

The flowing quality of each of the Chinese characters used in this book reflects the Zen contemplative ideal.

Fu (Buddha), page 4, written in *Tien-Shu* Celestial Script, Buddhist Charm Style

To Sit in Reflection, page 6, mystic Zen calligraphy written in *Lien Mien Ts'ao*, or One-Stroke Continuous, Style

Plan for Awakening, page 11, mystic Zen calligraphy written in *Lien Mien Ts'ao*, or One-Stroke Continuous, Style

Purity of the Way, page 21, mystic Zen calligraphy written in *Lien Mien Ts'ao*, or One-Stroke Continuous, Style

Jen (Benevolence), Sermon One, written in *Ts'ao-Shu* Grass Script

P'ing (Peace), Sermon Two, written in *Tien-Shu* Celestial Script

An (Tranquility), Sermon Three, written in *Tien-Shu* Celestial Script

The Whole Heart of Zen

The characters for Mind, Body, Hand, and Heart used throughout this book are written in *Tien-Shu* Celestial Script.

The author's seal chop on the previous page means "primal act of creation in a mystic state."

All calligraphy by Rev. John Bright-Fey